As They Grow

Your Two-Year-Old

W9-AHB-660

As They Grow

Your Two-Year-Old

By the Editors of **Parents** Magazine
and Diane O'Connell

St. Martin's Griffin **M** New York

Also by Parents Magazine:
The Parents Answer Book
Parents Magazine's It Worked for Me!
The Parents Party Book
Play and Learn
As They Grow: Your One-Year-Old
I Can Do It!: Physical Milestones for the First Twelve Months
I Can Do It!: Physical Milestones for One-Year-Olds
I Can Do It!: Physical Milestones for Two-Year-Olds
I Can Do It!: Physical Milestones for Three and Four-Year-Olds

A Roundtable Press Book

For Roundtable Press, Inc.:
Directors: Julie Merberg, Marsha Melnick, and Susan E. Meyer
Project editor: Meredith Wolf Schizer
Consultant: Marge Kennedy
Designer: Laura Smyth
Illustrator: Penny Carter

For Parents Magazine:
Editor-in-chief: Sally Lee
Senior editor: Betty S. Wong
G+J Director of Books and Licensing: Tammy Palazzo

ISBN 0-312-25371-0

First Edition: February 2000

10 9 8 7 6 5 4 3 2 1

Table of Contents

My many moods   60
Your two-year-old's emotional development

How I view the world   76
Your two-year-old's personality

Why I act the way I do — 96
Your two-year-old's behavior

It's potty time!   160
Your two-year-old and toilet-learning

Foreword

by Sally Lee

As the mother of a fun, inquisitive, loving two-year-old, I'm still trying to figure out why this stage is called the "terrible twos." I'd rather rename it the "terrific twos." Two is such an exciting age. Suddenly, that baby whose needs you catered to day and night has grown into a real little person—an individual with thoughts, opinions, and a will of her own. Now your child's verbal, social, and motor skills are developing by leaps and bounds. A two-year-old can express herself, is full of opinions, wants to show off her budding independence, and has a remarkable thirst for knowledge.

With this book, you can be your child's best teacher. We'll show you how to set safe limits when your toddler insists on doing everything herself; how to cope with the emotional roller coaster of a toddler's many mood swings; how to tame a tantrum and help your child try out potty skills. And best of all, how to take advantage of the many teachable moments that come with this age and stage. Toddlers just want to figure out how the world works; what a wonderful gift it is to be able to show them.

Let me go (hold me tight)!

Your two-year-old's quest for independence

When you hold a one-year-old in front of a mirror, she smiles. "Look at that adorable baby!" she may be thinking. Do the same thing with an older toddler and you'll still get a great big smile. But this time, that smile means, "Look at *me!* Aren't I adorable?" This is the beginning of your child's journey to becoming her own person, separate from her parents. And what a journey it is! By age two, your child is bursting with newfound skills—both physical and social—as she busily tests both herself and you.

What makes all this independence possible is your child's newly acquired physical prowess. Walking and grasping objects are now old hat, something she accomplished as a younger toddler. Now that those basic motor skills are behind her, she's ready and eager to take on more complex tasks. She can walk *and* carry an object in her hands. In fact, there may be times when she refuses to sit in her stroller, preferring to walk beside you while *she* pushes it. She can run, hop, climb, pedal, feed herself, and take off her clothes—something she will do with alarming speed, just as you've finished getting her dressed! And she can move away from you—often faster than you'd expect.

Your child's experiments with her physical abilities can seem amusingly perplexing (building a block tower only to knock it down) or downright dangerous (teetering on the edge of a chair as she reaches for something beyond her grasp). But what's going on in her mind is the process of discovering the meaning of independence: "If I can *build* a block tower, I can knock it down!"; "If I climb on that chair, maybe I can reach the box of cookies on the counter." When she knocks down the blocks, for instance, she learns that she has some power over her environment. When she climbs on the chair, she tests just how far her physical abilities can take her. She also learns that there are things she is capable of doing without you. In fact, "I can do it myself," could well be your child's anthem this year.

Two-year-olds aren't content to live off the scraps of independence their parents dole out to them. They want to be in charge of *everything* in their world: what they eat, what they wear, where they go, and what they do once they get there. It doesn't matter if it's 30 degrees and the ground is covered with snow: if your two-year-old wants to wear shorts and her favorite T-shirt, that's all the logic needed. She may see you engrossed in paying the bills, but if she wants you to play with her, "later" is not an option. She may suddenly turn up her nose at her favorite breakfast cereal and demand another brand. It's not that her tastes have changed; rather, it's the power to control her own environment that fuels her. Though she may not say so in words, her sentiments could be summed up with "I am the boss of the world!" She's not trying to oppose you. She simply expects you to share her viewpoint that she is the center of all things.

This enormous egocentricity is actually a good thing. It means that your child is developing a sense of herself as an individual with her own preferences and desires. In order to become her own person, she needs to check out just how much power she really has. To do this, she tests the limits to see how much you'll give in. This is a perfectly logical step; up until now, you've provided everything your child wanted or needed, and she learned to trust you and to believe that, in general, you will provide what she needs and wants.

Your child's struggle for independence is not simply a you-versus-me issue. She's just as hard on herself. Whereas younger toddlers learn to be oppositional as a way to start separating from their parents, a child in the middle twos begins to oppose even herself. When she was younger, if you offered her a red block, she would invariably want the blue block instead. Now, if she chooses the red block on her own, she immediately decides she wants the blue block. If she says "Yes" to something, it's almost immediately followed by a definite "No." Such contradictions may be hard to fathom, but they are actually a sign of growth. By exploring opposites and trying out different choices, she's learning to become an individual who can make her own decisions. Eventually she will be able to make a decision and stick with it.

SAFETY FIRST
Update your childproofing

A baby-proofed home isn't necessarily safe for your two-year-old. Your child's increased coordination can get her into more trouble than a one-year-old. She can open jars, get into the medicine cabinet, use a pair of scissors, and climb to new heights.

One of the most important safety rules to remember as you guide your child through this year is that just because she couldn't do something yesterday doesn't mean she won't be able to do it today. Because two-year-olds are physically capable of getting into more trouble than younger toddlers, now is the time to update your childproofing to prevent injuries and to allow your child the freedom to explore without you constantly having to steer her away from things she shouldn't touch. To update your childproofing:

• **Eliminate potential sources of danger.** Look at your home from your child's point of view— physically by getting down on your knees, and emotionally, by trying to figure out what might pique your child's curiosity. For instance, suppose you keep a heavy cookie canister on a shelf above the kitchen sink. Now imagine that you can see it from your child's height. You want

some cookies, but you can't reach them. What do you do? You pull over a chair and climb up, but you still can't reach it. So you stand on your tiptoes, and with some stretching, you can just about grasp it enough to move it forward—and it comes crashing down, causing you to lose your balance and fall.

This is how you must think in every area of your home, particularly the kitchen and bath, which hold the most potential sources of danger, including cleaning supplies, hot stoves, medicines, and drowning dangers. Staircases, doors, and sliding glass panels with outdoor access, electrical outlets, and windows and venetian blind or drapery cords also must all be considered potential areas of danger.

• **Be especially vigilant with your own behavior.** Because two-year-olds are impetuous, curious, and lacking in judgment, you need to be vigilant in supervising your child, no matter how safe you make your environment. It's crucial that you not allow your attention to become diverted when you're using household cleaning products, power tools, knives, or anything else that could pose a danger to your child. If, for instance, the doorbell rings while you're mopping the floor, don't leave your child unattended where she could have access to the bucket while you answer the door.

No matter how stressed, hurried, or distracted you are, you must stay particularly alert to danger. These are the times when you're likely to forget to put medicine back in a high cabinet, or to leave out a knife on the counter. A moment is all it takes for your two-year-old to find trouble.

It's important to set a good example yourself. Think of the message you send if you chew on a pencil, cross in the middle of the street or against the light, or fail to buckle your seatbelt. Your two-year-old finds great pleasure in imitating you and cannot differentiate between good and bad habits.

• **Teach your child to practice safe habits.** Begin to injury-proof your child by teaching her what's safe and what's not. While you probably already have begun introducing the warning "hot!," don't let this concept become taken for granted. Constantly remind your child of what's hot and what shouldn't be touched. That's especially true if you get a new appliance or when something new attracts your child's interest. Also teach her about sharp or pointy objects. When you use a knife, for instance, make sure you tell her that it's sharp and is not a toy. If you pretend to touch the tip and say "Ouch," that demonstrates your point in a more tangible way. Other safety concepts to begin teaching your child include water safety rules, warnings about putting things in her mouth that you haven't given her—especially if it's not food—and safety in crossing the street.

• **Express your safety concerns when your child visits others.** Because you can't completely control the environment when your child visits grandparents or other relatives and friends, you need to let them know what to keep in mind when you visit. But because you can't expect them to childproof their home as you would yours, focus on just a few main areas, such as the kitchen, stairs, and bath, and, during visits, limit your child to places that have been given the once-over. Never assume, however, that your child can, at this age, be left unsupervised for even a minute.

• **Encourage your child to explore.** For your child to gain confidence in her skills, she needs to be given the freedom to explore her environment—and even make some mistakes. Allow her to navigate the stairs while you're close enough to prevent a fall, for example. If she's safety monitored, her explorations will allow her to gain a sense of physical control, which in turn will aid her in her quest for independence.

A sense of ownership

"It's mine!" This statement, which your child will shout many times this year, pretty much sums up how she feels about the things around her. Her refusal to relinquish her grasp on a toy, or her use of the phrase as a greeting to a new playmate, is her way of setting the ground rules: "I'd like to play with you, but first you should know that this doll is mine, and I'm going to get very upset if you try to take it away from me." She may not even want to play with the toy herself, but it's important that she has control over its use.

The realization that something belongs to her and that she has a certain amount of control over how and when she uses it, and with whom she decides to share it (if at all), gives her a tremendous sense of power. It's really not so hard to imagine the impetus behind this seeming selfishness if you look back at your own feelings of possessiveness. Can you remember your first car and the pride of ownership you felt? In some ways, the car was an extension of who you were as an individual. It was a possession that you had control over. You no longer had to cajole your parents to give you the keys to *their* car. Imagine your response if the neighbor down the street said, "Hey, great car. Mind if I use it tonight to pick up my date?" Now imagine that your first car is your two-year-old's new dump truck and you have a pretty good idea of what it means to her.

Your two-year-old's favorite word

At age two, a favorite word creeps into your child's vocabulary. It's a tiny word, to be sure, but one that is loaded with significance in terms of her budding independence. That word, of course, is *no,* and it's usually said with a definitive brusqueness and a frequency that begins to approximate a mantra.

What's so important about this word? When a two-year-old says "No" she may not mean "No" literally. She's really expressing her desire to be her own person, separate from you. It's a way of figuring out who she is. Because her language skills are fairly limited at this age, "No" becomes the most effective tool for expressing herself. A typical two-year-old may even say "No" to something she wants to do or to have. So when you ask, "Would you like to go to the park?" and your two-year-old answers with a sharp "No!" she may actually be thinking, "Well, yes, I'd love to go to the park, but right now I'm playing with this sorting toy and I'm having fun and I'm not quite ready to stop. Let me see what happens if I put this red block into this slot. Then let's talk about going to the park." Of course, that would be a perfectly understandable response coming from an adult. She might mean, "Yes, this is something I'd like to do, but when the time suits me." You would respect that person for expressing her own individual desires. But the best tool your two-year-old has is the shorthand "No!" which can stand for many things.

CONFLICT
Independence versus ability

Imagine that you and your spouse are going out to a dance you've looked forward to for a while. When you arrive at the dance hall, you're told you must wear the hall's special shoes. Unfortunately, they're a half size too big and they weigh as much as construction boots. You try to dance anyway, but it's a catastrophe. You may have begun the evening with an image of yourself dancing gracefully across the floor, but the harder you try, the more you feel like a lumbering fool. Now you have a pretty good idea of the physical challenges your two-year-old faces.

Your child's curiosity and determination to explore are not always in sync with her actual abilities, and this can cause tremendous frustration. For one thing, two-year-olds are not as physically competent as they would like to believe they are. Their ability to imagine extends to being able to imagine themselves doing just about anything, including flying, driving the car, and whipping up a ten-course meal. Certainly, then, your two-year-old imagines that she can do things like running with an ease that may not yet match reality. Though most healthy twos can, indeed, run quite well, they are not able to coordinate their sight and forward motion smoothly, and consequently may trip and even run into walls.

It's not just her awkwardness with her large motor skills that can upset your child. Her lack of skill with her hands can be an enormous source of frustration as she tries to do or make something and it doesn't turn out as she expects. And so often she finds that she's limited in exercising her budding independence. She may be able to tell you what she wants for breakfast, but she still has to allow you to make it for her—and she must wait as you do so, which can be very frustrating.

The realization that she's incapable of doing as much as she wants to do can make her feel insecure and less capable than she really is. And often, her desires simply cannot be met. It isn't only her inability to do physical things that may frustrate her, though. Her independent streak may prevent her from wanting to follow your instructions.

Just as she's learned to express herself by saying "No," she also has to learn to listen to you when you say "No." Without the ability to learn from past experience and foresee the consequences of her actions, it may seem perfectly reasonable to your child to open the oven door and stand on it to reach a pot on the back burner! When you pull her away and tell her "No! That's dangerous!" she doesn't quite get why you're thwarting her ambitions.

Also, as she begins to form her own identity separate from you, she begins to realize that her parents are separate from *her* and have a relationship that does not include her. This realization can make her feel insecure and she may worry that you will not always be there for her. She may suddenly become clingy, fearing that when you leave, you may not return. Yet, she still has an intense need to know that the strong bond she has shared with you will continue to exist.

How it feels to be me

Only yesterday, it seems, I could barely walk across the room without falling flat on my bottom at least a couple of times. Now my arms and legs work really well and I can go everywhere! My hands can work so much better, too. Now, all those interesting things in my house are mine to explore. That pretty vase is almost within reach. Maybe if I pull over that chair and climb up on top, I can reach it. Then I can see what it really feels like. And I can get a better look at all the pretty designs.

Because I can do so much more now, I don't have to depend on Mommy and Daddy for everything. It used to make me feel so safe and loved to have them do everything for me. But now, I know I can do things for myself, and that makes me feel real proud. If I want to wear my red sweater instead of my blue one, I can! Sometimes I may say I want to wear the red sweater, but I don't really know what I want. It's just the very fact that I can say I want something that makes me say it. And that feels pretty powerful. Mommy and Daddy make all the big decisions, so whenever I can, I make a stand on some of the smaller things. Of course, all these choices can seem a little scary. There are times when even being given a simple choice, like what snack I want, can be more than I can handle and I get frustrated with myself and with you for not making the choice for me, the way you used to.

Sometimes I get afraid when you go to work and leave me at the day-care center or with a sitter. If I can make my own decisions and even run away from you in a crowded place, that must mean you can too. What if you decide not to come home? I need to know that you're still in charge, that you'll still take care of me. So, sometimes I want to run the show and make all my own decisions, and other times I want you to do things for me that I know how to do myself, like feed myself. And sometimes I just need to cuddle in your lap.

As I'm learning about who I am, I often find myself ordering adults around. But I'm not as sure of myself as I may seem, and mostly it's all bluster because the world is still such a scary place for me. If I can control just a small part of my world, it makes me feel more secure.

How your child's independence affects you

You may feel a mixture of joy and sadness as you delight in watching your child become independent and self-reliant, with her own desires, preferences, and abilities, while at the same time you learn to accept that she's no longer as dependent on you for every aspect of her life. There will be times when your child seeks the security that only you can provide. She may rush into your nurturing arms, desiring the comfort that can be found in the shelter of your lap. But more often than not, she will venture away from you into unchartered waters. Though it can be difficult to stand back and remain in the shadows, take comfort in the fact that your presence provides her with a secure base from which she can feel confident to explore and expand her newly discovered independence. She has a basic trust that you will not punish or reject her for going off on her own.

Your child's new ability to state what she wants may also be a mixed blessing for you. You'll most likely find yourself excited over her burgeoning communication skills, while at the same time you may worry about how much to give in to your child's demands. While you want to please her and encourage her in her quest for individuality, you may wonder whether giving in too often will turn your child into a tyrant.

Giving in to her demands to control other people's behavior will confuse her. After all, she needs you to be in charge even as she's making her demands. And if you do get into a habit of jumping when she says so, she's bound to push to find her limits, which will not serve her or you in the long term.

On the other hand, your child's bossiness at this age can even be amusing. When a two-year-old orders you to keep your eyes on the road while driving or tells a visiting relative to get out of "her seat" at the table, you may be tempted to laugh at such imperiousness coming from such a tiny person. Yet laughing may belittle your child. These orders are her attempts to be part of the world she lives in, as well as to have a sense of control over her own life. She may have heard your spouse, for instance, admonish you to keep your eyes on the road. And while she may not know exactly why, she does know that it's important. And if someone's sitting in her seat...well, it is *her* seat, after all. It's important to respect your child's needs while at the same time guiding her into more appropriate responses when you see her act in such a way that tramples on the feelings and wishes of others.

At other times, your two-year-old's attempts to become her own person will be downright scary. You may be terrified as you watch your child attempt a physical maneuver only a circus acrobat would try. While you do need to intervene when she's in danger, it's important not to overprotect your child from appropriate attempts at honing her skills. Too many "be carefuls" will undermine her natural sense of adventure and inhibit her from testing her wings as she should.

Your two-year-old's insistence on doing things her way can also cause you to become angry and frustrated with her. As you plead with her to wear her pretty new dress for Grandma's birthday instead of her favorite stained T-shirt, you may long for the days when getting her dressed was a simple affair. When you feel that there cannot be a choice on a particular occasion, approach these limits in another way. For instance, instead of asking whether she wants to wear this outfit or that one, ask, "Do you want to get dressed now or after you've had your snack?" This way, you're accepting and allowing her need for choice, without setting up a confrontation with her.

As your child struggles to conquer tasks that are challenging to her, you may also feel the urge to rush in and help her to solve every problem she confronts. But it's important not to allow those impulses to take over. For the first time in your child's life, she is striving to understand just how self-reliant she can be. How often and in what way you help her solve her problems will ultimately influence her own feelings about how competent she is. If she is trying to fit a puzzle piece in the wrong place, for instance, and you jump in and show her the right place, you may frustrate her attempts at figuring out how to solve a problem by herself. If you make such corrections often enough, she may eventually get the message that she's fundamentally incompetent. Rather, encourage your child by giving her feedback about her decisions so she can learn from the choices she has made. You might say, for instance, "Try turning the piece around and see if that works."

If your child says...	Do say	Don't say
"I don't want that cereal for breakfast."	"If you don't want this cereal, you can have [another brand]. Which would you like today?"	"You'll eat what I give you."
"No!" to a request to stop playing with something so she can go somewhere	"I can see you're having fun with that toy. If you like, you can bring it with you." Or: "You can play for five more minutes. I'll set the timer so you know when to stop."	"You'll stop playing when I tell you to."
"Stop working, Mommy. Play with me now."	"I'll bet you want to spend some time with me now. You pick out what we'll play, and I'll be done in a few minutes."	"Don't interrupt me while I'm working."
"I want to climb the monkey bars."	"I'll stand right here in case you need me to help you."	"You're too young. You'll hurt yourself."

The key to dealing with your own emotions as you watch your two-year-old's unbridled pursuit of independence and self-definition is to approach her with understanding and humor, and balance her need to do things her way with your need to be firm when necessary.

HELPING YOUR CHILD GROW
Nurturing independence

One of the best ways to support your child's emerging independence is to encourage her to make decisions and take on more responsibilities. Being able to make some choices and do things for herself will allow your child to have a growing sense of herself as a competent individual. Following are some suggestions for supporting and gently challenging your child's continuing quest for independence:

Limit your child's choices. If you ask your child, "Where would you like to go today?" the decision may seem overwhelming to her. Or she may come up with an entirely inappropriate response (such as, "The beach," in the dead of winter). Two-year-olds can manage making decisions better if they're offered a limited menu. Generally, asking your child to choose between two things will go a long way in giving her a sense of control and eliminating the possibility of her making an inappropriate choice. The key is to offer her choices that *you* can live with.

Avoid criticizing your child's choices. Suppose you've laid out two outfits for your child to choose from: a red-and-white striped shirt with red pants and a purple shirt with purple polka-dot pants. But instead of neatly choosing one whole outfit, your child says she wants to wear the red-and-white striped shirt with the purple polka-dot pants. If you tell her that she's made a bad choice or that the two items don't go together, you'll have defeated the purpose of giving her the opportunity to choose. Plus, she'll feel deflated. It's important to keep in mind that two-year-olds want to make decisions simply for the experience of choosing. It doesn't necessarily matter to them that their choices are "right."

Let go of the little things. Define for yourself what's a big deal and what's not. Allowing your child to decide small things that don't affect her health or safety will give her a sense of power and mastery. If she insists on wearing sunglasses at the dinner table, for instance, ask yourself if it's really worth a battle. Wearing the sunglasses may be her way of saying that she's different from you. If you give in on the little things, your child will be more apt to go along on the big things, such as holding your hand while you cross the street.

Give your child responsibility for small tasks. Encouraging your two-year-old to put on a sweater, return a toy to its proper place when she has finished playing with it, and set her own place at the dinner table (as you hand the items to her) will help give her a sense of growing competency.

You can also help ease her into bigger tasks by encouraging her to do part of a more complicated task. For instance, putting on a pair of socks can be enormously complicated for a two-year-old. But if you start the process by bunching them up and slipping them over your child's toes, she can pull them up the rest of the way. This process, of breaking down complex tasks into smaller components, allows children to feel that they are accomplished at many more activities and tasks than they would ordinarily.

Allow your child to be the leader on occasion. Let her choose which path to take to the park or let her make up the rules for a game. Avoid the impulse to tell her the "right" way to do something or to give her help she has not asked for. Two-year-olds will often have a plan of what they want to do, but because of their physical limitations, they may be unable to carry it out, and they need help in accomplishing their task. For instance, if your child is digging in the sand at the beach, she may want to pour water on the sand, but have a hard time maneuvering to fill the bucket with water as the tide rushes up on shore. You can guide her in holding the bucket and even carry it with her back to her sand project. But avoid doing it all yourself. And, by all means, allow her to wet the sand herself. In other words, you want to lend your assistance to *help* solve a problem—not to solve it yourself.

Applaud your child's process, not just the results. Your child may be struggling with a shape sorter, turning a square block this way and that, trying to figure out which of five holes it will fit in. Instead of waiting for her to figure it out before praising her, give her some positive feedback while she's working out the problem, saying something like, "I see you're really working hard at that. Good for you!" Similarly, if your child is trying to pour her own cereal, but she's getting as many flakes on the table as she is in her bowl, applaud her efforts at being able to open the box, pick it up, and pour out the contents. By focusing on what she's doing right, you give her the encouragement to take further steps toward independence. Be careful not to go overboard with praise, however, since you don't want your child to learn to explore new skills just to please you. Too much praise, ironically, can also lead your child to be fearful of trying new things if she worries that failing will lose your approval.

Set limits. The boundaries that you set on your child's behavior give her freedom to explore in safe and socially acceptable ways. *(For more on setting limits, see Chapter 6.)*

Toys and activities to enhance your child's independence
You can encourage your child's growing sense of independence by providing her with playthings and activities that help develop her physical capabilities as well as her sense of identity. Following are some suggestions:

♦ Climbing equipment helps promote physical coordination and can give your child a sense of competence.

◆ "Ride-on" vehicles also help to promote independence by giving your child another form of mobility.

◆ Child-size housekeeping toys, such as a make-believe stove or kitchen center; a play shopping cart and boxes of food; dishes, a broom, a dustpan, and so on, allow children to role-play and experiment with their identities.

◆ Baby dolls enable your child to be the mommy or the daddy and make all the decisions as well as practice nurturing skills.

◆ Dress-up clothes give children a chance to try on new identities. Superhero costumes, in particular, promote play that gives children the opportunity to fulfill their longing for control.

Listen to me!

Your two-year-old's communication skills

All through his early toddlerhood, your child absorbed an extraordinary amount of information about words. As he listened to adults and bigger kids around him, he began to distinguish different sounds and learned the meaning, rhythms, and patterns of speech. Though his own communication skills were limited to expressing one or two words at a time, he learned and absorbed all the information he needed to have real conversations.

Although all children develop at their own rate, by the time most children reach their second birthday, their language development really begins to take off. Each day, your child's vocabulary increases dramatically. Like a boulder rolling down a hill, his language skills gather momentum at a remarkable pace. Your two-year-old loves to name and label things, such as body parts, cars, animals, and plants. "What dis?" may be his most frequently repeated question.

Even more exciting than the sheer volume of words he has acquired is his newfound ability to form sentences and have a real conversation. In fact, by the end of his second year, your child may know as many as 1,000 words and be able to use five of them in a single sentence! This is nothing short of a language explosion. Imagine the learning and concentration that it took to reach this stage: first your child had to distinguish which sounds were words and which were not; then he had to associate those words with specific meanings; finally, he had to comprehend our language's grammar and structure.

DEVELOPMENTAL MILESTONE
Building language

Your two-year-old's construction of sentences occurs so smoothly and gradually you may barely notice his progression. At first, his sentences will be very simplistic: "Doggie play." But as the weeks and months progress, so do his communication skills. He adds words almost arithmetically. Soon he will form three-word sentences: "Billy play doggie." The meaning is clear, although your child is using only the most essential words to communicate. Gradually, he will begin to add articles, prepositions, and auxiliary words: "Billy play with doggie," "Billy play with nice doggie," or "Billy sit on doggie." He begins to have an understanding of tense and can speak about the past and future as well as the present: "Billy played with doggie" or "Billy want to play with doggie." He will also begin to use negatives beyond the simple "No": "Billy not want to play with doggie" or "Don't play with doggie." He may also use helping verbs: "Billy can pet doggie."

At this time, your child may begin to use pronouns, and will use them correctly most of the time. He understands that "he" can stand in for his brother and "she" for the girl across the street, and he correctly uses "we" when referring to more than one person and "you" when addressing you. Gradually, he refers to himself by pronoun rather than by his name. However, he will most likely refer to himself as "me," until the latter part of this year, when he begins to add the use of the pronoun "I." Your child can also tell you his full name. In fact, his name means a great deal to him as he begins to build up his own identity, and he will use it quite frequently.

With the complexities of the English language, your child will also accomplish another feat this year—the ability to distinguish between words that sound alike but have different meanings (too, to, two) and to understand that some words have more than one meaning (duck can be a command to crouch down or it can mean a bird on a lake).

Discovering the power of language

Much of your child's language ability is employed as a running commentary on his play: "I make the pasta now," "Here comes the choo-choo," "The cow goes in the barn." He will even talk to other children, although most of his conversation is directed first to himself and then to adults. He has begun to initiate conversation, unlike previously when he almost always spoke in response to a question or directive from an adult. Often, he'll begin a conversation by asking, "Why?" More than just seeking a flat out explanation of something, however, he knows that if he asks you "Why?" he'll get you to talk to him. He knows that talking is really important and he wants to do as much of it as he can. He learns that asking why is the best conversation starter there is.

Your two-year-old is also just beginning to discover the many uses of language. He knows that he can use words to express what he wants or needs: "Me want a peach." But beyond that, he has discovered he can use language to express ideas and information: "I don't like that," "That truck is big." He will use his newfound language skills to boast and brag about his other developing skills: "I can take my own coat off," "I climbed up all by myself," "Look what I made!" In fact, you will often hear his cries of "Watch this!" or "Look at me!" since language, as well as action, can now be used to draw your attention to him.

He will now use his language ability to manage his own behavior. If you warn him not to touch the oven door because it's hot, for instance, he will repeat your warning: "Hot! Don't touch." An older two-year-old finds that his words can manage others' behavior. He may tell a playmate "Mine!" if he wants to play with a toy. This is a long way from his earlier behavior of grabbing a toy or pushing a playmate to make his point. His language may take on a bossy edge as he commands adults: "Get out of my seat," or "Gimme that."

As your child nears the end of his second year, he'll begin to test out his understanding of grammar and usage. It may appear that he is taking a step backward when he says such things as "I eated all my corn," "I runned all the way," or "Look at all the mans." In fact, these "errors" show that he has learned some important principles of our language: that *ed* is added to words to put them in the past tense, and *s* is added to make a plural. He hasn't yet grasped, though, that many English verbs and nouns are irregular. Sometimes, for good measure, he may know the proper past tense of a verb, but still add an *ed,* resulting in such odd constructions as "wented" or "caughted." There's no need to correct your child. Simply continue modeling proper usage and your child will, in time, catch on.

Your child may have discovered the power of expressing himself though sound effects (crying "Zoom, zoom, zoom" when playing with a truck), chanting, or singing. Besides boosting his language development, singing helps him express feelings he doesn't yet have the words for. You may find that when your child sings, he seems more relaxed and uninhibited with using words. Even his pronunciation is better than when he is speaking. The most likely reason for this is that singing is more like playing (a "right-brain" activity) than communicating (a "left-brain" activity).

Your child's developing language skills have allowed him to make another giant leap in communication, as well—the ability to tell a joke. Of course, at this age, his jokes are usually fairly cryptic—you may not get what's so funny, but he sure does. His sense of humor most often centers on incongruity with one foot in reality and one foot in fantasy. The joke comes from associating those two different worlds. So, if he says, for instance, "The umbrella ate my soup," he recognizes the preposterousness of that event, and to him, that's a hilarious concept. Likewise, he'll find *your* jokes funny if they also center on the unexpected or incongruous. Putting a shoe on your hand and telling your child, "I'm putting on my mittens now," or asking him if he's seen your glasses when, in fact, they're on your nose, may elicit delighted peals of laughter.

CONFLICT
Getting the word out

A two-year-old's language development—while impressive to say the least—has not yet reached the point where he can express himself with verbal fluency all the time. In his excitement to share his ideas and observations, he may occasionally stumble over his words. He may run into the house, bursting to tell you about the beautiful monarch butterfly he saw, but all he may manage to get out is, "I saw...I saw...I saw..." Sometimes he can get so stuck that he may forget what he wanted to say altogether. Other times he has trouble pronouncing words correctly. His speech may be peppered with pauses, repetition of sounds and words, hesitations, and fill-in words like *um* or *uh*. He may become so overcome with emotion—such as when he's opening up presents—that he gets completely tongue-tied.

Known as "dysfluency," these glitches in speech tend to occur when your child's vocabulary is growing rapidly and when he is making the transition from single words to phrases and from phrases to sentences. Usually, these problems will not last for much longer than a few weeks. They are particularly apt to occur if he's feeling rushed, excited, upset, or just plain tired. During these times his mind is forming words faster than his tongue can produce them. And though no one knows why, dysfluency is four times more likely to occur in boys than in girls.

Your child may also have a difficult time expressing himself when he's angry. At such an emotional peak, it's not just dysfluency that may get in the way of his ability to communicate, but his inability to find the right words to express his feelings. Consequently, he may latch on to whatever negative phrase comes easiest and blurt out something like "I hate you!" when what he really means is "I don't like this situation."

The gap between what's on your child's mind and his ability to express his ideas will, on many occasions, frustrate and infuriate him. Your patience and encouragement will help him continue his forward march into the world of conversation.

Language and learning

Language and learning are thoroughly linked. Your child learns not just through his senses as he did earlier; now your explanations give him loads of information. He also uses language to tell you what he knows and to ask questions in order to learn more. But language still has its limits for your toddler. Likewise, the limits of his understanding about the world will show up in his use and misuse of words.

For instance, he may lump people, objects, and animals into broad categories. Thus, if the only animal he is familiar with is your pet dog, he may point to a neighbor's cat and say "Dog." And since he knows you as his "Mommy" or "Daddy," he may refer to other adults with these labels. Sometimes he may show that he knows there's a distinction between two things by adding a qualifier: If a dog is a "dog," and a cat is a "dog," the first time he sees a horse he may ask, "*Big* dog?"

Probably his biggest challenge in learning to express himself verbally is not being able to find the right word. In a language that consists of tens of thousands of words, having a vocabulary of only a few hundred to a thousand words can be severely limiting. He can become so frustrated when he realizes he doesn't have the words to express himself that he may simply dissolve in tears.

The hearing and language connection

As long as your child listens when others are talking, responds when you talk to him, and progressively understands more language, the fact that he may be acquiring words at a slow pace is not a cause for alarm. If your child seems to be especially slow in developing his language skills, however, it is possible that he may have a hearing problem, possibly caused by repeated ear infections or other illness.

Approximately three out of 100 children experience some degree of hearing impairment by the time they reach school age. If you think your child is not hearing properly, ask yourself the following questions:
• Does my child fail to respond when I speak to him from the side or from behind? (Some children are able to read lips and can understand more when facing the speaker.)
• Does my child *consistently* fail to respond when I speak softly to him?
• Does my child have difficulty following simple directions?
• Does my child fail to respond to music?
• Is my child unable to distinguish between words that sound similar, such as *feet* and *sheet* or *door* and *four*?
• Does my child give inappropriate answers to questions, such as answering, "Yes, more juice" to the question "Do you want to go to the park?"
• Does my child *consistently* turn the volume on the TV or tape player up too high or stand too close while listening?
• Does my child complain of pain or ringing in his ears, hold on to or cover his ears, or show other signs of ear pain?

If you've answered yes to one or more of the questions, have your child's hearing evaluated by your pediatrician, who may suggest a further evaluation by an audiologist. With proper treatment early on, most children can be helped to overcome the language deficit caused by hearing loss.

Sharing communication

The first time your child expressed his wishes in a sentence, both of you crossed a threshold of communication. No longer did you have to guess why he was upset, or where he hurt, or what he wanted. If he cried at being told you're going to visit the doctor, you could ask questions to find out why he was scared—and you could reassure him. He could ask *you* questions, too, and tell you what he's thinking.

As his ability to communicate grows, words give you a window into the way your child's mind works and his process of discovering the world around him. Most of all, you can actually have a real conversation! As you begin to share your own observations with him, you'll feel a deeper and stronger bond with him.

You may also feel the need to "do something" to help his language skills develop. But rest assured that your child will learn all he needs to express himself fluently without being formally taught. At this point, you'll naturally speak less "baby talk" to your child. This helps him learn new sentence structure and new words. But, imposing words on him out of context won't help him increase his vocabulary any sooner. Children learn words best when they can apply them to objects as they experience them. If a child is running his hand along a rough tree bark, for instance, he learns the word *rough* because he's experiencing the sensation.

You can help your child learn the names of things without forcing a lesson on him. For instance, suppose he's pointing to a toy he wants, but doesn't know its name. You can say, "Oh, you want the stuffed zebra." Now he has a name for the object. When you're out walking, follow his lead. If he stops to admire a flower, you might say, "Isn't that a pretty daisy?" At home, you can use everyday chores to help him learn the names of things: "Here's a spoon so you can eat your cereal." He doesn't need to repeat the words; he'll pick them up when he's ready. Talk frequently and naturally to your child; the more you engage him in conversation he enjoys, the better he will become at articulating his ideas and feelings.

In fact, being surrounded by adults who talk meaningfully to him is the best thing you can do to ensure that your child's communication skills develop fully. That especially goes for your child-care provider. If your child is left for long periods in the care of someone who either does not engage him in significant conversation or does not speak his native language and uses gestures to communicate, or has poor language skills, his language development could be seriously hampered.

How it feels to be me

When I see something new I get so excited. I want to know what its name is. Just yesterday I learned that the black box that sits on the kitchen counter and makes music is called a "radio" and that the big green bird my neighbor has is called a "parrot."

I can say so much now—not like when I was a baby and I couldn't say anything. I can tell my mommy that I want oatmeal for breakfast. And I can tell her that I want to wear my blue T-shirt when I go out. I can even tell her if my tummy hurts. But sometimes, there's so much I want to say and I can't make my mouth say the words. Other times it's because I don't even know what the words are. And sometimes it's because the words just won't come out.

Today, I played with a computer for the first time at my friend's house. When my mommy took me home, I was so excited, I wanted to tell her all the neat things it did. It talked and made noises and had lots and lots of buttons and bright colors. But all I could say was, "A 'puter. And...and...he can...he can..." I couldn't find the right words. My mommy was listening real hard, but I know she didn't know what I was trying to tell her. I tried again, but still my mouth couldn't get the words out the right way. I was so frustrated! And I got mad at myself. And then I didn't want to talk about anything. So I got real quiet.

Patience pays off

As exciting as your child's developing language skills can be, you may also feel some frustration because you can't always understand what he is saying or because he can't seem to get the words out. Be patient and tolerant of his mistakes. Let him know through your words and actions that you're interested in what he's saying. Get down to his level physically. Avoid asking him to slow down when he speaks or to repeat a word or start over. Simply say, "I'm listening" or repeat what he's said that you understand, such as, "You're telling me about Grandma's cat." When you take the pressure off, your child will find it easier to communicate with you.

When your child says such things as "I eated it all up," you may feel the need to correct his grammar. But it's important to fight the urge to correct him or to make him repeat it the "right" way, which could discourage him from wanting to communicate with you and from taking the verbal chances that allow conversation to flow freely. You can repeat your child's ideas, rephrased in the correct way: "That's right. You ate it all up." This way, you show him that you respect his developing language skills while helping him learn at his own pace. If your child is ready for the correction, he will note it and say it correctly the next time around. If he's not ready, however, he won't feel like he failed.

It's likely that you will understand what your child says far more than other adults do. If his grandmother has no idea what your child just said to her, for instance, act as translator by echoing his words. This will diffuse a mutually frustrating episode in which your child may not be able to make himself understood.

When children are learning the rules of their language, they often use amusing constructions or mispronunciations. It's important that you fight the urge to laugh at your child's mistakes. Language learning is serious business to a child, and he may take offense. If your child does utter something unintentionally funny, write it down in a journal so you can both laugh about it when your child is older and he can appreciate his early attempts.

Following are some common situations in which you may feel the urge to help your two-year-old improve his developing language skills, and recommendations for encouraging him and keeping him talking.

If your child...	Do say	Don't say
is grabbing for a coveted toy	"I like it better when you say please."	"Say please first."
says, "I sawed a rabbit"	"You saw a rabbit? What did it look like?"	"No. It's 'I *saw* a rabbit.'"
points to a fox in a natural history museum	"Look at that fox! What do you think it's doing?"	"That's a fox. Can you say 'fox?'"
excitedly tries to tell you about something but gets stuck on a word or can't get the words out	Nothing. Instead, get down to your child's level and listen patiently.	"Start over and speak slowly. I can't understand you."
says, "Me like sketti."	"I like spaghetti, too!"	"Me like sketti, too!"

The value of language in your relationship

Now that your child can communicate with words instead of actions, you can use his emerging language skills to help him interact with others in a positive way. If he's playing in a sandbox and gets into a hitting match with another child over the sand pail, you can say, "We don't hit. We say, 'Please can I have the pail?'" It's not likely that your child will be so polite the next time around, but he may say something like "Mine, now!" instead of using physical force against his playmate. You can also encourage him to use language when around other adults. When you see an acquaintance on the street, for instance, you might say to your child, "Adam, this is Mrs. Jones. Why don't you say 'hello' to her."

As much as your two-year-old is learning to communicate, so much more is going on in his comprehension of things than he is able to express. That's why it's important that you don't "dumb down" your own language to speak "on your child's level." You want to provide him with new things to say, and the best way to do that is to use your normal vocabulary as well as tone. Furthermore, it's no easier for a child to learn a babylike term for something ("quack-quack") than to learn its proper name ("duck"). And though his mispronunciations may be amusing, if you use them in your own speech, you'll only reinforce the incorrect pronunciation.

On the other hand, occasional episodes of silly talk or baby talk between you and your child certainly won't slow down his development. That also goes for his grandparents, who may still use baby talk with him. Baby talk will naturally start dwindling as your child understands more, though. The important thing to keep in mind is that your child will copy the speech patterns he's exposed to on a daily basis. If most of the time you engage him in lively, meaningful conversation, that's what he'll learn.

Language timetables

All children are on their own timetables when it comes to talking. Some children begin using words as early as 10 months of age; others will say little before age three. Boys, on average, begin speaking later than girls. Also, if your child has older siblings he may take longer to talk, either because he may not receive as much individual attention from you or because he can't "get a word in edgewise," or because his siblings

Did you know?
Albert Einstein was three years old before he started talking.

are such swift and skillful interpreters that he may not have much need to talk.

If your home is bilingual, or if you speak one language at home while another language is spoken at your child's day-care center, he also may be slower to begin talking because it will take him longer to learn two languages than to learn one. It's particularly important that you not confuse your child by speaking two languages to him yourself. If you want your child to learn both languages, however, you can have your spouse speak to him in one language exclusively while you speak the other language. Rest assured, however, that even if your child's language is delayed because of bilingualism, it will soon catch up—as long he is given plenty of one-to-one talking time.

It's important to keep in mind that language development does not reflect your child's intellectual ability. Rather, genetics are usually more responsible than intelligence. You may want to ask your parents if they remember when you began talking, and have your spouse do the same. It is likely that if you spoke early or late, your child will as well. But the bottom line is that it's not so important *when* your child begins to communicate but that he progresses in his skills.

HELPING YOUR CHILD GROW
Aiding communication

Children learn to converse fluently not by formal instruction but by everyday interactions that involve language. If you regularly talk—and listen—to your child, you're already doing much to help his communication skills. You can turn any place into a language-rich learning environment for your child.

Look for opportunities to make conversation. If you're driving somewhere with your child, use the sights you see along the way as a jumping off point for conversation: "Look at that red car. Where do you think it's going?" or "Who do you think lives in that house?"

If you're at the bank, use that as an opportunity for helping your child learn the names of things: *deposit slip, ATM card, bank teller, security guard,* and the denominations of bills. Supermarkets can provide endless labeling possibilities. On a walk to the park, remark on all the things and people you see: "There's a man pushing a baby stroller." "Look at that big truck." "Aren't the clouds fluffy today?" Daily chores also provide opportunities for your child to learn the words for simple concepts, such as *in* and *out, under* and *over, wet* and *dry.*

Play games that involve communication and expression. Games such as "office," "airplane," and "restaurant" provide a perfect setting for lots of back-and-forth talk. If your child gets stuck verbally, you can encourage him by asking questions. For instance, if you're playing restaurant and your child is the waiter, you can say, "What do *you* recommend for dinner tonight, waiter? Should I order the grilled cheese or the macaroni?"

Read aloud regularly. Picture books provide a wonderful opportunity for enriching language. They not only help to increase vocabulary, but also help your child to understand language patterns. Stories that use catchy rhymes and repetition are particularly good, especially ones where children can supply the words. But don't stop at simply reading the words on the page. Emphasize words that sound interesting, and have fun with rhythms and rhymes. Use the pictures to talk about the story and the things that are pictured. Ask your child to point to the kitten, for example, and speculate about how it got all wet. You might also encourage your child to make up his own stories.

Sing songs together. Singing is a fun, low-pressure way for children to practice new words and sounds. Songs with lots of repetition, such as "The Wheels on the Bus," help reinforce language skills and vocabulary. And don't worry about your singing ability—

or lack of it. Your child doesn't care how well you sing, as long as you're enjoying yourself. When you do sing, however, it's a good idea to raise your voice higher to make it easier for your child to match your pitch.

Ask lots of questions. Questions are a great way to spur language development—even if your child isn't able to supply an answer. When your child says something to you ("I throwed the ball") instead of simply restating what he's said, ask for more information: "What kind of ball was it? How far did you throw the ball? What sound did it make when it landed?" Be careful, though, not to put too much pressure on your child to supply an answer. The idea is to engage him, not test him.

Be a good listener. When your child says something to you, it's important that you give him your full attention. Don't continue to read the newspaper, watch TV, talk to someone else, or tell him, "Not now. Talk to Mommy later." If your child seems particularly excited about what he has to say and needs your complete attention, stop whatever you happen to be doing, get down on his level, look him in the eye, and listen to what he's trying to tell you. Most of the time, however, it's enough to let him know you're listening while you continue to go about your business. For instance, if you're making dinner and your child rushes in with a story, encourage him to tell it to you while you slice the carrots. Too much focus on his speech may make him too self-conscious or may even lead to his forgetting what it was he wanted to say. In any case, try not to interrupt or correct him.

Narrate your actions. Children learn new words by associating them with direct experiences. When you tell your child what you're doing, you let him see what you mean. For instance, when you give your child a bath: "Now we wash your neck...and your shoulders...and your back...and your knees..." When you dress or undress him: "Off with your socks...Pull your shirt over your head...Zip up your jacket...Tie your shoes." When you make dinner: "I'm chopping the carrots...Now I'm mashing the potatoes...I'm slicing the steak..."

Use more complex sentences. If your child says, "Look! Cat!" you can respond by saying, "Yes, there's a tabby cat. Would you like to pet it?" By expanding your child's simple sentences with more complex ones, you will help broaden his sense of how to use language.

Set aside special conversation time. Make this private time just between the two of you so that he has the benefit of your undivided attention. Follow his lead instead of trying to impose the direction of the conversation. Two-year-olds will tend to speak more freely when they're expressing their own ideas. This is also a good opportunity to learn what's on his mind.

Make language fun. Language doesn't always have to be "correct" or even make sense for children to learn. Silly word games, nonsensical rhymes, and bad puns delight children and facilitate a healthy love of language.

Look for toys that encourage language development. Tape recorders specially made for children can inspire your child to record himself telling stories or singing songs. Listening to his voice played back can give him a big thrill and act as encouragement. Toys made for pretend play, such as a barnyard set, a play kitchen, a cash register, and pretend food, encourage children to talk out make-believe scenarios. "Talking" books (electronic books that "read" the text aloud) give your child added "read to" time and help him learn to develop listening skills.

Toys to enhance your child's language

♦ Sesame Street Elmo's Talking CD Player (Fisher-Price)

♦ Sesame Street Talking Alphabet (Fisher-Price)

♦ Barney Song Magic Banjo (Playskool)

♦ Blue's Clues, Steve's Press & Guess (Fisher-Price)

♦ *Rhinoceros Tap—and 14 Other Seriously Silly Songs.* Performed by Adam Bryant with Michael Ford (Workman, 1996). Comes with an audio tape and accompanying book, illustrated by Sandra Boynton.

♦ *If You Give a Mouse a Cookie* by Laura Joffe Numeroff, illustrated by Felicia Bond. Songs performed by Carol Kane (HarperCollins Juvenile, 1994). Audio cassette with songs, games, and readings and accompanying storybook.

♦ *Chicka Chicka Boom Boom.* Book by Bill Martin, Jr., and John Archambault, illustrated by Lois Ehlert. Audio cassette performed by Ray Charles (Little Simon, 1991). An invitation to memorize the 26 letters of the alphabet.

♦ *Rock 'n Learn Phonics* by Brad Caudle and Richard Caudle (Rock 'n Learn, Inc., 1992). Audio cassette and book, illustrated by Bart Harlan.

Watch me learn!

Your two-year-old's intellectual growth

Your two-year-old runs her hands along a bumpy concrete wall. She stomps her feet into puddles, seeing how high she can make the water splash. She crouches down and watches ants with the intensity of a scientist viewing slides under a microscope. She yanks a leaf off a bush and smells it.

She bangs a stick rhythmically against an empty bucket. She fills a bucket with sand, then empties it out. Then does it again. And again. She flicks a light switch on and off—twenty times. She carefully constructs a tower of blocks, only to knock it down.

These actions may look random, unconnected, and even silly, but they are actually serious business. Your two-year-old is using all her senses—sometimes exhaustingly so—to figure out the world around her. For two-year-olds, the world in all its wonder comes into focus in Technicolor™ glory, and they want to know *everything* about it. They seek that knowledge by exploring and experimenting, playing and pretending, sorting and categorizing, doing the same thing over and over again, and asking sometimes seemingly endless questions.

DEVELOPMENTAL MILESTONE
Play with a purpose

Before your child turned two, she explored her world by picking up objects, putting them in her mouth, and dropping them. This was her way of learning about the objects, albeit in the most rudimentary way. Sometimes she did these things simply for the sake of doing them and because it was fun. Now when she picks up something, she has a *purpose:* "What can I do with this?" she seems to be asking. She'll squeeze, poke, drop, shake, pull apart, and suck on an object—all in her quest to learn everything she can about it. She is a natural-born scientist, delighting in the wonder of her newfound discoveries.

These discoveries are the first stages toward grasping the abstract concepts and physical properties of objects that adults simply take for granted. When your two-year-old builds a bridge made of blocks, for instance, she learns, through trial and error, that she must use two blocks of the same height to form the bridge's foundation. Though she does not yet understand the abstract concept of "equal," she discovers what will happen when the blocks *are* equal—and what will happen when they're not. It's the next step from when she dropped a block as a one-year-old and discovered the laws of gravity. But this is more complex and requires her careful thought and attention.

She learns that when she tips over a cup of water, she gets wet. When she does the same thing with a cup of sand, she doesn't. She can't explain to you the difference between liquids and solids, but she's learning about these properties all the same. When she discovers that round things like balls and oranges roll, but square things like blocks and books do not, she's learning basic geometry. And when she pours a large cup of water into a smaller cup, the overflowing water teaches your child about the concepts of volume and flow. But for now, it's just fun for her to watch the water spill over.

Give a two-year-old a basket of multicolored blocks or plastic figures and watch what happens. She will almost immediately begin sorting them: red blocks here, blue blocks there; big people here, little people there. She is beginning to show her understanding of how things are alike and how they differ. Likewise, when she fits together a puzzle of large, simple pieces, she learns about size and shape.

As she learns to distinguish between colors, sizes, and shapes, she begins to learn about the different properties of her toys. She knows, for instance, that a truck is not a good thing to hug when she's sad, but that her doll will give her comfort. She can't explain why, but somewhere she has the understanding that a doll stands for a person, in addition to being more cuddly than a truck.

Though she is beginning to distinguish the various properties of different objects, her level of discrimination is still severely limited. For instance, she knows that if she throws a plastic cup, it will fall to the floor and nothing much will happen. But if she's only been allowed to hold an unbreakable cup, she doesn't know that if she picks up a glass and throws it that it will break. To her, the properties of a cup consist of its shape and function—not of its material.

The role of physical development in learning

At the age of two, the combination of fine motor skills and cognitive development allows children not only to make connections between things, but to act on them as well. For instance, when a child picks up a square block and tries to put it into a square hole, she has to do more than match shapes. Unlike a circle, the sides of a square must be aligned properly if the block is going to fit. A one-year-old might get frustrated easily and try to pound the peg in. A two-and-a-half-year-old, on the other hand, understands that the corners need to be lined up before she can make the block fit. Not only that, she now has the fine motor control to act on that discovery.

Your two-year-old's greater fine motor skills also mean that she can put crayon or pencil to paper to achieve certain desired results. This is a major leap, for now she can begin to express her experiences through drawing, while at the same time learning the properties of art materials. As she pushes and drags a crayon across the page, forming scribbles, she learns not only what the crayon can do, but how she can control the motion in her arm and hand. She learns that she can make thick lines with a crayon—each one a different color!—and that she can poke holes through her drawing paper with the pointy end of a pencil.

Younger two-year-olds are neither capable of nor interested in making "real things." It is beyond their understanding now that a circle might stand for a sun or a circle with "limbs" sticking out of it stands for a person. Instead, their excitement and learning comes from making something that didn't exist before: a blank piece of paper is now filled with colorful scribbles. As your child gets closer to age three, she will begin to make lines that have a purpose, as well as create specific forms, the first usually being a crude circle. She may repeat this circular form over and over, joining these circles with lines and dots and even blotting them out with masses of scribbles. As your child's motor control becomes further refined, she will begin to isolate forms, repeat them, and join them. Once she masters this step, she will begin to create pictures that represent specific things to her. Though you may not be able to decipher her images, she may proudly proclaim, "This is our house. Here's you making supper." This is an exciting stage in drawing—your child has made the connection that marks on a page can stand for something. This ability is the earliest precursor to learning to read.

Checking your child's vision

Two-year-olds are rarely able to tell their parents if they have trouble seeing. Even if they could express themselves, it's not likely that they would even know that such a problem exists. If images are fuzzy to them, well…that must be the way they are.

It's up to you to watch for any signs that your child may have a vision problem. Keep in mind that the following symptoms can indicate normal two-year-old behavior. A child with a vision problem, on the other hand, will *consistently* engage in one or more of the following behaviors. If you answer yes to any of the following questions, have your child's eyes checked by a doctor:

- Does my child fail to notice or recognize objects or people either nearby or at a distance?
- Does my child squint or scrunch up her face when performing close tasks?
- Does my child tilt her head to one side when examining something?
- Does my child avoid any activities that call for good vision, such as looking at books?
- Does my child sit too close to the TV or hold books or objects very close to her face when looking at them?
- Does my child have difficulty distinguishing colors?
- Do my child's eyes appear to move rapidly, as though dancing?
- Is my child unusually clumsy?
- Does one of my child's eyes turn in or out, or do both eyes appear crossed?
- Does my child complain of having a headache or nausea or seeing double after doing close work?

The use of routines

The amount of information a two-year-old learns in a single day can be enormous. All this experimenting and exploring creates in her an intense desire for order. That's why routines and rituals are so important; they help a child "place" the information, give her a sense of predictability, and help her to conserve mental energy. Imagine if everything were to be new to her every day; she'd be exhausted from sensory overload! On the other hand, if she knows she always puts on her shirt before her pants, that's one less thing for her to have to learn.

As hard as it may be to believe, the same child who leaves a path of chaos in her wake as she touches, rearranges, and overturns every new object she comes in contact with will also demand rigid order and predictability in other areas of her life. Plastic figures must be lined up in exactly the same way each time; clothes must be put on in a precise order; and don't even think of leaving a step out of your child's elaborately constructed bedtime or bath routine!

These routines, while offering your child predictability and security, also help her learn about time and sequence. Although she can't yet read a clock, she knows what "naptime," "dinner-time," "bathtime," and "bedtime" mean, and she knows that certain activities accompany each of these daily events. She's also learning what comes before and after. She knows that bathtime comes first, and then storytime, and then bedtime. And though she doesn't yet understand the concepts of "later" and "in an hour," she does understand "after dinner" and "after your nap." When she gets dressed, she learns about sequence: "First my shirt, then my pants, then my socks, and last, my shoes."

Why ask "why?"

Usually at around the time a child turns two-and-a-half, her deep curiosity about the world and desire to converse with you combine to produce "the why phase." The questions may seem endless: "Why is the grass green?" "Why do birds chirp?" But children this age are not seeking scientific, detailed answers. In fact, they usually don't even know yet what the word *why* means, and they certainly don't understand the concept of cause and effect when it concerns anything more complicated than knowing that if she drops something it will fall down. "Why" can actually mean "how" or "what" or "when." Asking "why" is the best tool a two-year-old has for trying to find out more about her world. She is trying to make a connection between something she experiences and her ideas about it. Your responses to her questions help her to arrange and rearrange what she thinks.

While your two-year-old wants to know more about something, she doesn't yet have the ability to start a conversation. Asking "why" gives her that entry. Chances are, she doesn't really want to know "Why it go 'rroooom' " when you start the lawn mower. She just wants to know more about the lawn mower in general. Plus, she knows that talking is a good thing because adults do it all the time. Asking you "Why?" over and over is her way of keeping you talking to her.

Early math

Your two-year-old may amaze you with her ability to rattle off numbers. Indeed, it's not uncommon for children this age to be able to count as high as 20, particularly in a sing-song kind of way. But such an ability, while impressive in itself, does not mean that your child has attained a basic understanding of numbers or numeric concepts. In fact, she may skip around quite a bit in her counting, leaving off large blocks of numbers or counting the same number several times ("One, two, three, six, ten, three, four, seven..."). Being able to recite numbers does, however, provide her with the correct names for numbers and put them in her memory for later on.

Most two-year-olds understand the difference between the concepts of one and two. Three, however, is a harder concept to grasp. They understand absolutes, such as *big* and *small,* but don't understand gradations in size, such as *big, bigger,* and *biggest.* They also are not yet able to distinguish quantities if their forms are not identical. For instance, if you give two children one cookie each but break one of those cookies into two pieces, the child with the whole cookie will think she has less. Furthermore, nearly all two-year-olds simply don't understand counting as a process of addition, although when they put all their stuffed animals into a single pile, they are experimenting with the basic idea of quantities.

How make-believe play helps learning

Your child's use of pretend play helps her to learn more about the world. While she may not ask you questions about an upcoming doctor visit, for example, she may enact a "visit" through playacting. She may give her stuffed bear an injection with a pencil. She may check his heartbeat by pressing a cup against his chest. She may test his reflexes by banging him from head to toe with a plastic hammer. She may cast herself as the patient, the mommy, and the doctor, and play all three parts simultaneously. In this way, she can "live through" or take control of a situation that she doesn't yet fully understand and which may frighten her.

While pretend play may appear to be little more than your child simply amusing herself, it's one of the most crucial steps in her learning process. This kind of play allows her to build up her confidence, face her worries and fears, come up with new ideas, and expand her understanding of how the world works. It's also a way for her to work out her relationships with the people in her life—mother, father, siblings, baby-sitter, doctor. When she pretends to be these people, she explores both how she feels about them and develops an understanding of how they interact with her. Pretend play also lets your child manage her emotions. (*For more on emotional development, see Chapter 4.*)

Engaging in fantasy play marks a great leap forward in your child's cognitive abilities. When she makes a block stand in for a sandwich she serves to her doll, for instance, she shows an understanding that one thing can represent another. Like her developing artwork, this use of symbolism also acts as a precursor to understanding the abstract concepts of letters and numbers. All of this exploration gives your child a sense of competence, which in turn will help her to feel more confident as she learns the letters, numbers, colors, and shapes that make up the world. Finally, pretend play gives your child the opportunity to solve problems. If she invites three dolls to her tea party, but has only two chairs, she must come up with a solution to accommodate her guests. Such problem-solving abilities will serve her well later on, when she needs to solve math problems or think critically about a story.

CONFLICT
The limits of understanding

Your two-year-old's growing cognitive abilities are often ahead of physical abilities, which can lead her to make mistakes in her judgments. Two-year-olds, for instance, are just beginning to learn the meaning of opposites, including "come and go," "near and far," and "fast and slow." Yet because their vision is not fully developed, they have particular trouble with the concepts of "near and far." If your child is looking at a picture on a shelf and then looks away, she may have trouble finding the picture again. For this reason, children like to grasp and hold on to objects to learn about them more fully. It's also why they'll always place a glass near the edge of a table, where it's closest to their line of vision. Of course, they will invariably knock the glass off the table because their peripheral vision is still not developed. They simply do not see the glass if it is not directly in front of them.

Your two-year-old's memory is also not yet fully developed, and can be highly selective. She'll remember a place you took her to a week ago, she'll remember the name of a new playmate she met yesterday, she'll remember the words to a song, but she may forget something you told her not five minutes before. She'll need to be constantly reminded about the little step down between the kitchen and the living room that keeps tripping her up.

Just as her memory is still highly selective, so is her ability to anticipate consequences. She may be able to figure out that you're leaving because of the keys in your hand and the kind of shoes you're wearing, but that forethought doesn't extend to her own behavior. She may climb up a stepladder without ever giving a thought as to how she might get down. And though she has been scolded time and time again not to play with the buttons on the VCR, when she sees those buttons today, the memory of past scoldings and anticipation of a new one is nowhere on her mind. Until her day-to-day memory improves, it's best to keep items your child finds intriguing—but that you don't want her to get her hands on—either way out of her reach or out of sight.

How it feels to be me

I am playing at my new friend's house. She has so many pretty and interesting things! Things I've never seen before. I want to find out everything about them. There's a box with pretty pictures on it. I want to open it to see what's inside. Wow! It plays music! When I close the lid, the music stops. I open it again and on comes the music. I do it again…and the same thing happens!

Oh, look! Over in the corner is a bright orange ball. It's got funny little bumps all over it. What does that feels like, I wonder? I pick up the ball and run my hand over the bumps. They feel funny and make me smile. Then I squeeze the ball. I wonder what it tastes like? I bite down on it. Not much of a taste. I drop the ball and it bounces. Then it rolls away under the bed.

On the table next to my friend's bed is a round thing with numbers on it. I wonder what it is? I pick it up. It's heavier than the ball. I pull at different parts of it, but it doesn't open. What could it possibly do? Maybe if I shake it, it'll make music like that box! Nope. It only makes a tiny rattling sound. If I drop it, maybe it'll bounce like the bumpy ball. Oops! I guess not.

Children learn in ways that may not always make sense to adults. Their learning process can also try a parent's patience.

If your child...	Do say	Don't say
insists on playing with a play phone as though it were a truck	"Wow! Look at that truck. What else can you do with the phone?"	"Let Mommy show you the right way to play with this."
has been banging a wooden spoon against a pot for the last quarter of an hour	"That spoon makes quite a sound. Let's see what kind of sound it will make if we bang it on the carpet."	"Why don't you go play with something quiet for a while?"
runs out of ideas while playing "grocery store"	"What do you think should happen next?" If your child doesn't respond, then say, "Remember when we went to the grocery store? What did we do after?"	"I know! Why don't we put the groceries away?"
spills while trying to pour juice in a cup from a large container	"That juice container is too big for you. Let me pour the juice into this small pitcher. Then we can practice pouring the juice together."	"Look at the mess you made! Don't try to pour juice yourself."

Keeping up with each other

The explosive learning that goes on from age two to three can be wondrous for you as well as for your child. Suddenly you see the world through your child's eyes, and everything becomes new and exciting. But you may also find yourself exhausted and exasperated by your child's intellectual development. The first time your child asks "Why?" is a momentous occasion; by the thousandth time, you may feel worn down. If your child wants to know why her eyes are brown, instead of launching into an explanation of genetics, talk about different eye colors of different family members. Rather than responding to your child's "why" questions as a demand for a precise explanation, think of them as a springboard for a conversation between you and your child. It'll relieve you of pressure and be more informative overall for your child.

Likewise, when your child asks you to read *Goodnight Moon* to her for the umpteenth time, you may feel more like howling at the moon than reading the Margaret Wise Brown classic yet again. It may help to keep in mind that faced with the daily onslaught of new information, having a little repetition in her day can be a source of comfort to your child. At least she has something she's familiar with and that she knows! It may help to remember that she won't insist on hearing the same story every night forever.

You may feel pressured to "do something special" to help foster your two-year-old's intellectual development. You may feel as though you have to provide your child with "educational" toys and make playtime a learning experience. Relax! Your child will learn everything she needs to learn so long as you provide her with a stimulating and loving environment. In fact, trying to force "learning" on your child may have the opposite effect. Simply supporting and encouraging your child's sense of discovery can do more for her intellectual development than any kind of formal learning experience. And the added benefit of a more relaxed approach is that your own sense of discovery will be renewed.

The "natural" way to increase your child's knowledge

The natural world provides myriad opportunities for your child to learn more about her environment. Children are innately curious about every new thing they come in contact with. A nature walk is a great way for children to discover and learn firsthand about the world around them.

As you walk, simply and spontaneously name things: "Don't those ants look busy?"; "Look way up high in that tree. Do you see the cardinal? What a pretty bird"; "I hear the brook gurgling. Can you hear it, too?" Talk about colors: "Look how pink this flower is"; "That leaf is dark green. This one is light green"; "That butterfly is the same color as your shirt—orange." Point out shapes that resemble other shapes: "This rock is round, like your red ball." All of this will help sharpen her ability to perceive, as well as help her to see the relationships among things.

Your child's natural curiosity will prompt her to interact with her environment. She may pick up a branch and poke it in the ground or swipe it at a bush. She may try to yank some flowers out of the ground. She may want to throw pebbles into a stream.

Monitor her actions for her own—and others'—safety, and to make sure she doesn't damage the environment, but in a way that doesn't cut off her joy of discovery. For instance, instead of admonishing, "Leave that alone" and pulling her away from a flower she is trying to pull up, tell her, "We shouldn't pull up flowers that don't belong to us. But you can smell it or touch it."

HELPING YOUR CHILD GROW
Adding to your child's discoveries

Nearly everything your child comes in contact with will help her to develop her intellectual growth. You don't need to give your child "lessons" or do anything formal to foster her learning process— *everything* is a learning experience to a two-year-old! Here are some ideas for making the most of your interactions with your child and the materials she encounters.

Look for toys that offer a range of play activities. Toys that are designed for one use only, such as make-believe phones or cash registers allow for only limited play opportunities. The more ways your child can play with a toy, the more "educational" it will be. When choosing toys for your child, look for those items that can be used in a variety of ways and that encourage children to use their own imagination. Toys that come in sets, such as a barn with animals, a farmer, and a tractor, for instance, will inspire your child to play in a fuller, more inventive way than would a few animals alone.

Provide your child with materials that inspire creativity. Any safe object that your child can handle can be considered educational. In fact, ordinary household objects such as paper towel tubes and plastic containers make great toys because children will use their imaginations to re-create these objects into one-of-a-kind toys. If your child rolls a toy car through a towel tube, that's a toy. If she wads up a paper towel and stuffs it in the tube, she can stop the car from rolling through. She has now made a more complex toy. Other ordinary objects, such as wooden spoons, plastic food containers, and pots and pans can help her have fun sorting the objects and grouping them together. And never underestimate the educational play value of an empty shoe box, which with your child's imagination can be a doll bed, a barn for play horses, a silly shoe, and a thousand other things.

Avoid showing your child the "correct" way to use something. It's okay to show your child how a toy works when introducing it for the first time. After that, however, let her use the toy in whatever way she chooses. She'll learn more by giving her imagination free rein than she will by adhering to a set of instructions.

Support your child's fantasy play. If your child asks you to join in her play, follow her lead. Let her decide what your role will be and what she wants you to do. On the other hand, if your child doesn't ask you to join in, it's best not to intrude or you may be asking your child to give up her control. If she runs out of ideas during her play, avoid the temptation to supply her with suggestions. Instead, use questions to provoke ideas, such as, "What do you think should happen next?"

Engage your child in counting games. Games and rhymes that isolate fingers or toes, such as "This Little Piggy," or counting other body parts such as ears or elbows help children begin to develop an understanding of the relationship of objects to numbers. Also, because children are so attuned to their bodies and senses, they're apt to learn these concepts more quickly than if simply counting objects. When you're setting the table, you help your child learn one-to-one relationship concepts, as well as counting. For instance, you might say to your child, "Each person gets one napkin. There's you—that's one. There's me—that's two. And there's Daddy—that's three." Then, as you help your child place the napkins, "One, two, three napkins."

Use everyday chores and routines as learning opportunities. Sorting laundry provides a great opportunity for learning to group like objects together: towels over here, T-shirts over there. Socks, especially, can help your child learn to identify colors and to match them accordingly. Bathtime is a perfect time for encouraging natural investigations into concepts such as quantity and volume. Just be sure to have several different-sized containers for your child to fill and empty. While on outings, point out and name familiar shapes to your child, such as circles, squares, or triangles.

Make reading time enjoyable for your child. If reading time is playful, your child gets the message that books are fun, and you'll help instill a lifelong love of learning. It's important that you avoid making reading into a lesson or something that your child "should" do. Let her choose the books she wants you to read to her. If she has trouble deciding, give her several books to choose from. When you sit down to read with her, allow her to set the pace. Keep in mind that two-year-olds often are not interested in reading books the traditional way. Your child may stop frequently to ask you questions. She may skip ahead several pages. She may have no interest in the story line but will be fascinated by the pictures. Follow her lead. If she asks questions, use that as an opportunity to talk. If she skips ahead, or has no interest in the story line, don't insist that she go back. The important thing is that reading time doesn't turn into lesson time.

And don't just stop at books. Use interesting pictures from magazines, newspapers, and junk mail to inspire your child to make up stories. You can even write down her stories and help her make her own book.

Provide balance in play opportunities. Children need a variety of experiences and changes in scene to develop their learning. If your child is basically homebound most of the time, either in day care or at your own house, make sure you balance this experience with outdoor play. Regular trips to a park will give your child a whole different range of experiences. Even mundane outings, such as a trip to the grocery store or the laundromat can be interesting to your child. On the other hand, children who spend a good amount of time outdoors need to have that tempered with indoor play. And if your child is around other children for most of the day, look for opportunities for quiet, reflective time. The more your child's time at home is balanced with venturing out into the world, the more interests you help develop in your child, and the more she will learn about the world, and herself.

My many moods

Your two-year-old's emotional development

As your toddler turns two, you may be pleasantly surprised by the relative calm in his moods. Where before he was often upset by his lack of abilities, becoming tearful and whiny, now he seems more serene and sweet tempered. Life does not seem to frustrate him as much and he is not ruled so much by his emotions as he was just a few months before. Along with this newfound emotional stability, he may begin to express his deep love for his parents, both verbally ("Me love Daddy") and through cuddling and affectionate kisses and hugs.

But the first six months after turning two are merely the calm before the storm. While each child's development may vary by as much as six months, usually by the time a child reaches age two-and-a-half, his emotional reactions to the world around him may seem over the top and completely unpredictable. One moment he may explode in anger and frustration, the next he may dissolve into a fit of giggles. He may lovingly crawl into your lap looking for some cuddles one minute, only to push you away in anger several minutes later. While this kind of behavior in an adult would seem truly bizarre, in a two-year-old it's perfectly normal and signals an important developmental leap. Not only is your child making huge strides in the development of his sense of self and in his language skills, but he is now beginning to develop an emotional vocabulary. Just as he has learned to say "I love you," he has also learned to say "I hate you."

When he was younger, his ability to communicate his feelings was severely hampered not only by his lack of language skills, but by his limited emotional responses. Crying, in short, was his main tool for expressing how he felt. If he was hungry or tired, he cried. If he did not want his play interrupted to go to bed, he cried. If he was refused a toy, he cried. If his cries did not lead to the response he was looking for, he resorted to screaming and thrashing.

Though as a one-year-old, your child had a full range of emotions from sadness to elation, from fearless to frightened, those emotions are now more nuanced and somewhat less extreme. He can feel a little frightened, but not be overwhelmed by fear. He can feel friendship toward another, rather than simply love or trepidation. And his improved communication skills help him express his understanding of emotions in words: "Love you," "Me not like dat," "Me happy," "I scared."

At this age, your child will also express his feelings through symbolic behavior. He may show tenderness by putting a bandage on a stuffed bear to cure a boo-boo. He may demonstrate rage by picking up a toy truck and hurling it against the wall. He may reveal his own sadness by trying to cheer up a favorite doll.

He may also make symbolic gestures that don't initially appear related to his emotions. For instance, a two-and-a-half-year-old whose beloved pet turtle dies may take the news surprisingly calmly. He may not even seem to understand what you've told him, but later he may dump the turtle's food and paraphernalia and anything else associated with the turtle, such as books or a stuffed toy, into a heap on the floor. While this may seem like a strange way to express grief, it's not all that different from an adult's behavior of ripping up or tossing out souvenirs or photos from a spurned lover.

DEVELOPMENTAL MILESTONE
The beginning of empathy

Not only has your two-year-old begun to tune in to his *own* emotions, but he can now sense what others are feeling as well. He's knows if Mommy is "sad" or if a playmate is "mad." Another child's crying may trigger his own tears. He may pat the head of an injured playmate in a gesture of comfort. He may want to know why you look sad and try in his own way to cheer you up by offering you a favorite toy or giving you a big kiss. By responding to others in these ways, your child demonstrates that his perspective of the world is branching out; just as he is learning to recognize his own emotions, he can put himself in another's shoes.

This beginning of empathy is a major leap forward in a child's development, a result of his burgeoning sense of self. Only when a child is able to see himself as a separate being can he begin to recognize that others are individuals, too. It begins to dawn on him that "If I feel sad sometimes, maybe Mommy does, too," or "If I scream when I'm mad, then when my playmate screams, she must be mad."

Oh, those mood swings!

A two-year-old's moods often seem to be on a roller-coaster ride, going from the highs of infinite joy to the lows of devastating sadness or anger. The reason for these wild mood swings is that, at this age, your child is caught between two stages of life: the helplessness of infancy and the relative independence of later childhood. He now has increased communication skills to express his desires, improved motor skills to get around, a sense of himself as an individual apart from his parents, and an improved understanding of the world around him. But his abilities are still very limited, and it's those limitations that cause the mood swings.

For instance, because your child's sense of time is still mainly limited to the present, telling him he cannot have a desired treat now is the same as telling him he can never have it, which may upset him. (Just imagine if someone said you can never eat another piece of chocolate for as long as you lived...or see another movie...or get together with a beloved friend. You'd be pretty upset, too!) A two-year-old has not yet developed a sense of sequence, so when you strap him into a car seat to go on a trip to the park, he may become angry at being restrained, forgetting that this is just one of the steps necessary to having a good time.

A study of 140 toddlers ranging in age from one year to nearly three (conducted by Wendy S. Grolnick, Ph.D., an associate professor of psychology at Clark University in Worcester, Massachusetts) demonstrated the frustrations of these kinds of limitations. The children, who were in a playroom with their mothers, were each shown a snack or a wrapped gift by a researcher, who then told the children she had to leave for a few minutes but would give it to them when she returned. She placed the object out of reach and left the room for up to six minutes. As expected, most of the children were upset, but the difference in how they recovered varied by age. The youngest children quickly forgot about the desired object. The oldest ones were able to use their reasoning and verbal skills to assist their waiting, often saying such things as, "Okay, when the lady comes back, I'll get to open the present." However, the younger two-year-olds' memories were developed enough that they could not forget about the present or snack, yet their verbal skills and reasoning ability were not sufficiently developed to understand that they would get the treat eventually, and they could not soothe themselves successfully.

If your child's anger seems excessive

While it's normal for two-year-olds to hit, kick, or shove others in anger, some children lash out for no apparent reason. They may not even appear to be upset after these outbursts and, if asked, cannot tell you why they expressed outrage. Sometimes a child's excessive anger is in response to stresses from a life event. Ask yourself the following questions to try to determine the source of his emotions:

- Has there been a change in your child's life, such as a move, the birth of a sibling, or new child-care arrangements?
- Have you been experiencing marital difficulties? (Sometimes a child's anger reflects his worry over tension between his parents.)
- Have you or your spouse or other close family member suffered a lengthy illness?
- Have you or your spouse recently been away from your child for a long period of time, such as for a vacation or business trip?

If the above issues do not seem relevant to your child's behavior, you may want to take a look at your style of parenting. Sometimes children act aggressively as a way of getting their parent's attention. Others do it as a way of getting their parents to set some limits on their behavior. *(For more information on aggressive behavior and how to handle it, see Chapter 6.)*

Further, if none of the above situations applies to your child, you've reevaluated your parenting style to no avail, and you still can't get at the source of his anger, you should consult a professional to see if his anger is a symptom of a psychological disorder. If not dealt with now, while your child is young, anger can become worse and lead to other behavioral problems later on.

Anger and jealousy

For the first time, your two-year-old may demonstrate anger over ideas, which is more complex than the simpler anger that grew out of frustration felt earlier in his life. This simple frustration of being two—the straddling of independence and helplessness—can be enough to cause your child to go into a fit of anger. Suppose your child is straining to reach a toy that's just out of his grasp. His face is scrunched up with the effort as his fingers wriggle furiously toward the toy. As a one-year-old, his frustration and anger were focused on his inability to reach the toy. Now, something else enters the picture. Wanting to help, you pick up the toy and hand it to your child, but instead of pleasing him, you've made him *really* angry and he bursts into tears and shoves the toy away. What happened? You've interrupted his idea of getting the toy. A less frustrating approach might be to ask if your child wants your help before assisting him.

Jealousy, too, is experienced differently by the two-year-old. Because of his emerging independence, it begins to dawn on him that he is not always at the center of his parents' lives. Often, a new sibling will prompt these feelings of jealousy. When you're nursing the baby, your two-year-old may try to pry the baby away, saying, "I want your milk, too, Mommy!" If you're simply holding the baby on your lap, he may demand that you put the baby down, claiming, "That's *my* lap!" But a new baby isn't the only cause for his jealousy. He may try to separate you and your spouse if he sees you kissing or hugging. He may be unable to bear any attention you give an older sibling, creating a distraction to bring the attention back to himself. Unlike last year, your child can remember his feelings of jealousy and may carry those feelings over beyond the actual event that caused his jealousy. For instance, last year he was returned to contentment when you hugged him immediately following hugging your spouse. This year, he may retain some resentment toward your spouse for having hugged you an hour ago.

The root of this jealousy stems from his fear that he will lose your love. Losing a parent's love is terrifying to any child, but it's particularly devastating to a two-year-old because his beginning sense of personal identity is still so fragile and largely defined by his relationship with his parents. If he loses your love, he feels as though he's losing a part of himself. Because he does not yet have the communication skills to say, "Don't forget about me—I'm important, too," his only way of showing this fear is through negative attention-getting behavior, such as tantrums, hitting, tears, and even biting.

As difficult as it is to be around an angry two-year-old, it's important that you let your child work through his anger—within the parameters of acceptable behavior, of course—as well as help him identify what it is he's feeling.

If your child...	Do say	Don't say
cries because a playmate snatched his toy	"I know you're angry. It's upsetting when someone takes your toy."	"Oh, don't cry, honey. It's only a toy."
throws a tantrum in a store because you won't buy him a trinket	"I can see you're angry with me because I won't buy you that toy. Would you like to tell me how angry you are? That might help you feel better."	"What on earth is wrong with you?"
hits his baby sister because he's angry that she's getting your attention	"I understand why you're mad. It's okay to be angry, but you can't hurt the baby. That's not okay."	"Don't you ever hit your sister again."

Handling emotions

There is so much that your two-year-old can now do that he couldn't do before, but handling his many emotions is not one of them. Because two-year-olds do not yet have the ability to identify their feelings and desires through specific words and requests, they often resort to behaviors that seem incongruent. For example, they may express elation through frenzied activity, crying, or even falling asleep as much as through giggles and smiles. If your child bursts into tears upon arriving at a friend's birthday party it's not that much different from an adult crying with elation at a wedding or upon receiving a sentimental gift.

All this inability to moderate his emotions may cause your child to become easily exhausted, resulting in whining and fussing. Because his communication skills are still not fully developed, this is the only way he has of telling you that he's frustrated or overtired.

The conflict for your child comes from your increased expectations for his behavior. Now that he can talk, you expect that he will choose words rather than simple physical activity to express himself. But, once overtaken by emotion, your two-year-old relies on the tried and true means of letting you know how he feels, which is by acting out. He may feel frustrated at his inability to state his case verbally and may even be ashamed of his actions. The trouble, of course, is that he can't always control himself.

How your child's moods affect you

You may find yourself accompanying your child on his roller-coaster ride of moods. Your own intense anger, frustration, and fear may become heightened as you respond to your child's behavior. You may feel disturbed by these feelings and even begin to doubt your fitness as a parent. But it may be comforting to know that virtually all parents experience these emotions. It's perfectly normal to have these feelings. Just because you are now experiencing some negative emotions toward your child does not mean that you love him any less.

The first time your child says "I hate you!" you'll feel like all the care and love you've given him is being thrown back at you. You may even want to scream back, "I don't like you either!" Instead, keep in mind that your child does not mean this personally. It's important that you keep your own emotions in check. It can be frightening to a child to see his parents out of control. You need to reassure your child that you still love him and to help him feel secure by giving him the attention he needs while at the same time setting limits on his behavior. Take a deep breath and say, "I know you're angry. I still love you." Besides helping to deflect some of his rage, this lets him know that you respect his feelings.

At other times, you might find your child's angry outbursts comical. But keep your amusement to yourself. Laughing at your child's expression of anger or jealousy sends him the message that his feelings don't matter and, worse, are silly.

You may feel the need to "fix" your child's moods. It's distressing to see your child dissolve in tears of sadness or punch a toy in anger. But telling a child not to be sad or mad or jumping in to "save" him from experiencing such negative feelings teaches him that it's wrong to have those emotions. Such a reaction would also give him the message, however subtly, that he can't handle his own feelings and that the only remedy is for you to take over. Instead, let him know that it's okay to feel whatever he's feeling and allow him to find his own methods for soothing himself.

By accepting all of your child's emotions, you lay the groundwork for how he views his own emotional life. Dismissing a child's feelings or trying to sugarcoat them in the hope that they'll go away, on the other hand, sends him the message that he can't trust his feelings and he will learn to doubt his own judgment. Eventually, he may lose confidence in himself. The only way to dissipate negative emotions is for children to talk about them, name them, and feel understood.

Keep in mind that this emotionally volatile stage will soon come to an end. Two-year-olds have extreme emotional reactions because they see things in black and white and because they do not yet have the reasoning skills to moderate their reactions. By age three, with your help and guidance, your child will develop the coping skills that will help him be more cooperative and more in charge of his own feelings. In the meantime, remember that coping with your two-year-old's emotional ups and downs is terrific training for when he reaches his teens!

How it feels to be me

When I'm upset, I need you to be calm and reassuring. Sometimes my fury frightens me. I don't know where all these bad feelings are coming from and I feel like a top spinning out of control! If you start yelling back at me, then I feel really scared because it seems like my whole world is falling apart. And if you tell me not to be so mad, it makes me even madder. How can I not be angry if that's what I feel? It's times like this, when I'm feeling angry or jealous, that I really need to know you love me more than ever. I need to know that everything's going to be okay.

Giving your child an emotional vocabulary

Helping a two-year-old name his feelings promotes secure relationships. When he can think about feelings and ideas and understand both what he and others are experiencing, he can form bonds with others. When he can name his emotions and understand how to manage them, he'll get along better with friends, have stronger social skills, and experience fewer negative and more positive emotions. He may still become angry or sad, but he'll be better able to soothe himself and bounce back from distress. Giving your child words for his emotions helps him feel that not only do you understand what he's feeling, but that it's okay to feel the way he does. Here are some suggestions for helping your child learn about his emotions:

Sing a song. Remember the song "If You're Happy and You Know It?" This is a perfect song to help your child learn to identify emotions. Introduce different emotions into each verse (for instance, "If you're angry and you know it, say 'I'm mad'"). Then ask your child what kinds of things make him feel that way. Make sure to take your turn, as well. Tell your child what makes you excited, sad, or angry. By learning more about what makes you feel certain things, your child can learn more about himself.

Use stories as a springboard for talking about emotions. As you read to your child, talk about what the characters are feeling and why. *(See "Books about feelings," pp. 74–75.)*

Encourage your child to use art materials to express how he feels. Pounding clay or coloring on big pieces of paper can provide a physical release for negative emotions. Older two-year-olds may use art materials to tell a story about the event or problem that triggered certain feelings.

Set limits on your child's behavior. It's important for your child to know that it's okay to have negative emotions. However, you do need to make it clear that you will not tolerate any destructive, aggressive, or dangerous behavior.

Help your child to find positive responses to his negative emotions. Instead of simply punishing him for acting aggressively out of anger, help your child work out a solution to the problem that triggered the anger. For instance, say, "You may be angry that your friend took your pail and shovel away from you. It's okay to be angry. But it's not okay to hit him. What can you do instead?"

Take advantage of teachable moments. Children learn best when you talk about feelings as they arise naturally in the course of daily events, as in "I feel so relaxed and calm sitting in this park," or "I'm sorry I embarrassed you by telling Aunt Janet what you said yesterday." This will also help foster a close relationship between you and your child. But be careful not to overdo it by turning such sharing into an intellectual exercise. You want your child to *experience* emotions more than being concerned with simply labeling them.

Encourage fantasy play. Through make-believe play, your child can find a safe venue for expressing even the most intense emotions. If he's angry at a playmate, pretending to be a superhero will help him vent his anger in a way that harms no one. Such play also gives your child the opportunity to develop methods of controlling himself that he'll be able to use throughout his life. Additionally, fantasy play allows children the opportunity to try out a wide range of emotions: a boy can express tenderness toward a doll or a girl can scold her imaginary playmates as she deals with issues of right and wrong in a way that gives her some power.

Show your child through indirect ways that you understand what he's feeling. You don't always have to label an emotion to show your child that you understand what he's feeling. If he's banging on pots and pans as you're trying to put the new baby to bed, you don't need to stop what you're doing and say, "I know you feel left out." Instead, say "After I put the baby to sleep we can read a book together." He'll get the message that you understand what he's going through.

Don't force your child to talk about his emotions. There will be times when your child prefers not to talk about what he's going through. Show him you respect his feelings by not insisting he talk about them.

Cutting down on angry outbursts
While there's nothing wrong with your child feeling angry some-times, it's not an emotion that you want to dominate his life. But because so much is out of their control, two-year-olds often become furious at circumstances that older children will naturally take in stride. It's up to you to try to avoid those situations that will cause him to feel frustrated, jealous, and out of control, as much as possible.

Be flexible with routines. While it's important for two-year-olds to have routines, sometimes children just don't want to do some-thing the way it's usually done. If you insist that your child stick to the routine, you'll only be setting yourself up for a battle of wills. Occasionally altering the routine is not going to do your child any harm and may head off a temper tantrum. Skipping a bath one evening because your child balked is not going to undo established routines, as long as you don't allow his balking to dictate the rou-tine each night.

Always have an alternative up your sleeve. Sometimes distraction is the best way to stop your child from spiraling into a fit of anger or frustration. A toy, a book, or a new and interesting item may be just the diversion needed. Sometimes a material distraction is not possible and you'll need to use your creativity to help your child turn his attention elsewhere. Look around you and see if there are any sights that may capture his interest, such as a person walking a dog, a brightly painted truck or sign, or a group of children playing nearby.

Watch for your child's cues. Not all of your child's mood swings are as sudden as you may think. Most children give out signals that a storm is brewing: a tapping foot, a clenched fist, a furrowed brow. When you see these cues, figure out what might be causing your child distress and see if you can help him deal with the problem before it causes a meltdown.

Make sure your child is well-rested and well-fed. Children—as well as most adults—have a difficult time controlling their emotions when they're hungry or tired. Make sure to build a rest period and snacks into each day.

Counteracting jealousy

Jealous behavior is often an attention-getting ploy. When a new sibling comes along, for instance, a child may feel as though he's no longer as important in your life. When he sees you and your spouse showing affection for one another, he may feel left out. Your first response when your child shows jealousy should be to comfort him and show him that you understand his feelings.

If your child's jealousy has resulted in destructive behavior, then you'll need to help him to understand that it is not acceptable for him to behave that way. If your child throws his toys at the wall because he's jealous of the gifts a relative brought for the new baby, tell him clearly that you know he feels left out when his baby sister receives a gift, but that he is not to break or hit things. This is more effective than simply insisting that he stop being jealous. Still, feeling understood doesn't always make the jealousy disappear. Telling your child that there's enough love to go around, for instance, is too abstract a concept for him to understand. Instead, *show* him that he's still special and important by spending time alone with him every day.

If his jealousy is caused by a new sibling, it's also a good idea to give him some small responsibility so he feels like an important part of the baby's life. When children feel jealous, it's often because they don't feel as valued as they used to. Asking your child to help pick out the baby's clothes or to assist you in giving the baby a bath will make him feel important and less excluded. However, don't insist that he stick to those responsibilities if he doesn't want to. Finally, one way to help head off jealousy before it even begins is how you tell your child about the impending birth. Saying, "I'm having another baby," may inadvertently send him the message that he's not enough for you or worse, that he's being replaced. Instead, tell him, "You're getting a sister or brother." This may reduce his anxiety level because he won't feel as though his place in the family is being usurped. Refrain from asking if he wants a brother or sister or how he feels about the upcoming event, since he's likely to reject the idea outright, and asking his opinion isn't really fair to him.

Books about feelings

While most books can provide opportunities for discussing the characters' feelings, the following books particularly deal with emotions with which two-year-olds can identify:

♦ *The Happy Day* by Ruth Kruss, illustrated by Marc Simont (HarperTrophy, 1989).

- *I Don't Want to Go* by Anne Sibley O'Brien (Henry Holt, 1986).

- *A Baby Sister for Frances* and *A Birthday for Frances* by Russell Hoban, illustrated by Lillian Hoban (HarperTrophy, 1993 and 1994).

- *Big Al* by Andrew Clements, illustrated by Yoshi (Aladdin Paperbacks, 1997).

- *Edward Loses His Teddy Bear* by Michaela Morgan, illustrated by Sue Porter (Dutton, 1988).

- *Feelings* by Aliki (Greenwillow, 1986).

- *Mean Soup* by Betsy Everitt (Harcourt Brace & Company, 1992).

- *Nana Upstairs & Nana Downstairs* by Tomie dePaola (Viking, 1987).

- *Noisy Nora* by Rosemary Wells (Dial Books for Young Readers, 1997).

- *On Mother's Lap* by Ann Herbert Scott, illustrated by Glo Coalson (Clarion Books, 1992).

- *Peter's Chair* by Ezra Jack Keats (Puffin, 1998).

- *When I'm Afraid, When I'm Angry, When I'm Jealous,* and *When I'm Sad* by Jane Aaron (Golden Books, 1998).

How I view the world

Your two-year-old's personality

What was your two-year-old like when she was a baby? Did she adapt easily to whatever circumstances she found herself in? Was she fussy and irregular in her bodily functions? Did she cry inconsolably for seemingly no reason at all? Was she highly active, able to crawl herself into trouble inside a second? Was she timid around others? Or was she gregarious?

If you look back at your child's early behavior, chances are her reactions to circumstances and people around her haven't changed much. In fact, from the time a child is born her personality is clearly evident. As children approach age two and begin to develop their language and motor skills, as well as a sense of independence, their behavior style—or temperament—grows more clear. For example, a baby who cried inconsolably for seemingly no reason at all may turn into an intense two-year-old who throws frequent tantrums.

DEVELOPMENTAL MILESTONE
The emergence of personality

An understanding of different personality types comes from New York University psychiatry professors Stella Chess, M.D., and Alexander Thomas, M.D., who pioneered the most important study of temperament. By closely observing a group of 136 children from birth through young adulthood, Chess and Thomas were able to identify nine different dimensions of temperament, involving activity level, regularity of biological rhythms, response to new situations, adaptability to change, intensity of response, sensitivity to stimulation, quality of mood (positive or negative), distractibility, and persistence in pursuing a goal. Through their observations, they were able to show that a child's inborn temperamental traits had a great effect in determining his or her overall behavior.

Because it is somewhat cumbersome to keep track of nine categories, Chess and Thomas looked for certain combinations of traits that tended to recur in the children they studied. They found three clusters that were particularly common. These groups of behavior make up the categories known as easy, slow to warm up, and challenging. Further research led to the inclusion of a fourth category—active.

It's important to point out that most children do not fall neatly into any one category. And while basic temperament tends to remain constant, the behaviors that a child exhibits can change. For example, some children may be more timid at certain stages of their lives and more outgoing at other times. Likewise, an easy two-year-old may act out and become difficult when she enters school. Keep in mind also that the following types are not intended to serve as labels. They are merely ways of helping you to understand your child and how she relates to her environment. By learning a little more about your child's unique personality, you can better understand her behavior, what drives it, and how to help her maximize the best features of her personality while minimizing those aspects that are less desirable.

The easy child

Some children seem to be consistently in a good mood. They greet the world with a smile on their face, they adapt to new situations easily and without complaint, and their sleeping and eating patterns are regular and consistent. They readily join in playgroups and get along well with other children. When they do have a tantrum, it is often mild and short-lived. If your child is easygoing, you know that taking her on errands or an outing is a pleasure because she takes an interest in her surroundings and can be counted on to adapt to whatever situation she happens to be in.

An easy child's responses tend to be moderate. Give her a gift she's been longing for and her face will light up and she may show genuine delight, but she won't shriek with pleasure. When a playmate yanks her favorite toy away from her, she may simply whimper. Even her reaction to pain is moderate. If she falls and cuts herself, she will more than likely cry quietly rather than howl in pain. Some easy children may not even register dismay, smiling even when they are in anguish.

Because easy children are so flexible and compliant, it's easy to overlook any distress they may be in and to push them beyond what they can comfortably tolerate. For instance, a two-year-old who never complains as she accompanies her mother on errand after errand may actually be exhausted and in need of rest. A child who puts on a brave face during a vaccination may not be willing to let on that she's in pain and needs her parent's comfort. And a child who has overheard her parents tell others, "She never gives me one ounce of trouble," may feel under tremendous pressure to meet those expectations, at the risk of not expressing her anger, fear, or any other negative emotion. She also may find it difficult to stand up for herself, allowing others to take advantage of her. Therefore, it is important to pay close attention to your easy child's needs. Just because she isn't clamoring for your attention does not mean she doesn't need it.

The slow-to-warm-up child

The slow-to-warm-up child hangs back when entering a new situation, clutching or hiding behind her mother's legs. This reticence may lead others to label her "shy," although that label doesn't reflect what's really going on. The slow-to-warm-up child simply needs more time than others to assess new situations. By observing from the sidelines, she gathers and processes information—information crucial to her before she plunges into a new activity.

While other children learn about new experiences with their hands or by contact with others, a slow-to-warm-up child learns first with her eyes, by observing what is going on around her. She may linger on the sidelines, watching from the safety of her mother's lap as other children play. Though she is not yet participating directly, she is practicing the activity in her mind until she feels ready to join in. But once she joins in, she plays with as much gusto and has as much fun as her more outgoing peers.

Did you know?
Most people have felt shy at some point in their lives. In fact, one study (by Philip Zimbardo, Ph.D., of Stanford University) revealed that only about 10 percent of adult Americans claim they've never felt shy.

The slow-to-warm-up child tends to be less active than other two-year-olds, and her responses tend to be moderate—unless she is pushed to join an activity or new situation before she feels she's ready. Then she may break down in tears, heaving great sobs or howling because it's just much more than she can endure.

At home, the slow-to-warm-up child needs predictability in her routines. She doesn't like change, and will need time to adjust to any deviation. She may even be timid with relatives who are not frequent visitors. Grandparents who visit a few times a year, for instance, will need to give your child time to reacquaint herself with them before she feels fully comfortable.

Shyness does have its advantages. The slow-to-warm-up child will tend to be more sensitive to others' feelings, paying attention to the nuances of behavior that other children miss. She will be less apt to plunge ahead into potentially dangerous situations. And, as she gets older, she will choose her relationships very carefully. Such discernment will reward her with close, loyal friendships.

While most children go through some shyness at one point or another, only about 15 percent are actually born with a shy temperament, according to parenting expert Jerome Kagan. And even though this timidity is part of their inborn nature, about half will outgrow this predisposition by the time they are age six. Only about 25 percent of the original group will remain shy for their entire lives.

The challenging child
While all two-year-olds are challenging to a degree, the truly challenging child's demeanor is over the top. Think of any behavior a child exhibits, and the challenging child demonstrates it to the utmost. Her joy is boundless and her despair seemingly endless. She will shriek with joy over a small gift, she will shower her parents with hugs and kisses, she may seem to be forever in motion, and she can be more stubborn than a pack of mules.

The challenging child has trouble adapting to new situations, her biological functions are often unpredictable, she may wake up grumpy and frequently be in a bad mood, and she's hard to please. When she's upset, she can be almost inconsolable. And while all two-year-olds assert their independence through contrariness, she will become downright defiant. You may get her dressed to go somewhere special, but just as you're getting ready to leave, she may tear off her clothes and refuse to put them back on. You may get her successfully buckled in her safety seat only to have her wriggle out of it when you're on the highway. She may have extreme reactions to minor upsets: a stain on her favorite shirt or a different kind of juice than she's used to may be all that's necessary to send her into a full-fledged tantrum.

All this intensity can be positive, too. When the challenging child is having fun, she may express her pleasure through squeals and peals of laughter. She can be more affectionate than other children, showering her loved ones with spontaneous hugs or kisses. Her sensitivity allows her to notice things other two-year-olds aren't aware of, making her an interesting companion. And challenging children will hardly ever fade into the woodwork. The sheer force of their dynamic personalities commands attention from others.

If you find that your child's tantrums are more intense, last longer, and are more frequent, you might want to talk to your child's pediatrician, who can either reassure you that your child's behavior is well within the normal range, or if not, may recommend that you seek appropriate intervention.

The active child
Two-year-olds and activity certainly go together, but the energy level of an active two-year-old could probably light up a city. An active child can have an underlying easy or challenging disposition, but is basically ruled by the need to keep going, to run when walking would do. She will climb anything "because it is there." Given lots of space to run around in and permission to flit from one activity to the next, the active child will be cooperative. Try to rein her in, and she'll respond in a challenging, difficult way. Keeping her safe will be your primary challenge, as will—unless you're the active type yourself—simply keeping up with her.

As she grows, the active child will be able to accomplish much—if she can stick to any activity long enough before being distracted by another equally interesting pursuit.

Pleasing you and still being herself

It's rare that a parent's temperament is completely compatible with that of a child's, so conflicts over behavioral style are bound to occur. And therein lies the challenge for your child. Your child wants nothing more than to make you happy, but often her natural impulses are at odds with your expectations. And this confuses her. She may not understand why you are impatient or angry with her. After all, she's behaving in the only way she knows how.

Let's say you have a challenging child and she's used to having her sandwich cut into four triangles. Then one day you accidentally cut her sandwich into four squares. This is not a change that pleases her. She wants her sandwich the way she always has it and she begins to wail. If you become exasperated with her and tell her that you're not going to make another sandwich and she's just going to have to eat that one, she simply can't understand why *you're* so upset. In her eyes, *she* was the one who was wronged. She doesn't want you to be angry with her, but she also doesn't know how to tell you that she can't help feeling upset herself.

Or let's say you have a slow-to-warm-up child who's clinging desperately to your legs at a family reunion. You hate to admit it, but you feel a little embarrassed over your child's timidity and, frankly, you'd like to show her off to those relatives who haven't seen her since she was a little baby. You're very proud of your child and you know how delightful she can be. But she's not making much of an impression right now. So you grow a little frustrated with her and maybe you crouch down and look her in the eye and say, "Please say hello to your Great Uncle Al. He's not going to bite you, you know." But your child doesn't know why you're angry with her. She needs a lot of time to feel comfortable in this situation. She really does want to join in, but it just doesn't feel right to her to step forward and look this big stranger in the face and say "Hello." It makes much more sense to her to observe her uncle (and everyone else at this party) first so she can feel a little more at ease with him, and *then* say hello. To her, this behavior makes perfect sense.

Suppose your child is highly active. It's dinnertime. Your child has eaten everything on her plate, and in record time. But you and your spouse are still eating and you expect her to stay at the dinner table until everyone is finished. Well, this is going to be agony for her! Every nerve in her body is crying out to move. She can't understand why she must sit still. It's like disobeying the natural laws of her own body. And so she feels highly conflicted. She does not want her parents to be mad at her, but she also can't stifle her need to exercise her body.

Setting up playdates for your two-year-old

Two-year-olds benefit tremendously from exposure to other kids. Getting together with peers strengthens their social skills, increases their use of language, and is just plain fun. Matching children by temperament—or at least understanding the impact of personalities on get-togethers—can help make your child's playdates more successful.

Easy children will likely fit in well with a variety of other children. Your toddler and her playmate may comfortably do some things together, then move apart to do their own activities. Offer different things to do, such as paper to scribble or paint on, clay, a tent made out of a blanket draped over chairs, and plastic dishes or blocks to stack, dump, and bang on. If the playdate is outdoors, allow the children to seek their own activities as long as they are appropriate, safe, and well supervised. As easy as your child is, be prepared for some disagreements over toys if more than one child wants something. Twos do not understand the concept of sharing, although an easy child may give in more quickly. When the children start competing for things, try to distract them with other activities. If nothing seems to work, it may be time to end the playdate since one or both children are probably tired.

Slow-to-warm-up children need time to observe before joining the action. If your child is slow to warm up, encourage her to play with other children without pushing her into a group. When arranging a playdate, you may want to choose children who are a little younger than she is if she needs more confidence, or a year or two older if she is more of a follower. Make sure that playmates have similar temperaments to your child. For example, if your child is quiet and laid-back, she probably will be most comfortable with another child who is much like she is. A more aggressive child might scare and upset her. Don't be discouraged if your child spends a good part of, if not the whole first playdate making sure that you are close by. Just allow her to watch as long as she wants. You might also try to get her interested by first finding a toy or a book you know she will like and playing with her yourself. When she's ready to join other children, let her go. If she doesn't, don't worry. You may be surprised at the next playdate when she joins in immediately.

Challenging children need more direct help in learning to get along with other kids. If your child is challenging, you probably will want to choose a more easygoing playmate who will be less upset by complaints and sudden changes in mood. It's also recommended that you set up the playdate with a child she has already met before, if possible. Like a slow-to-warm-up child, it's probably best to limit playdates to one other child, or a small group if the playdate is outside. An active group may tend to overstimulate your child, which may result in her collapsing in tears or a tantrum at the slightest upset.

Prepare your child in advance for a playdate. Talk about your plans, where you will go, or who will be coming over. Discuss some activities and see how she reacts. Then stick to your plans as much as possible to avoid sudden changes that your child would have difficulty adjusting to. You may want to plan activities with paints, water, clay, and crayons and paper, rather than providing toys that may be fought over.

How it feels to be me

A common situation, such as a birthday party, will prompt very different feelings and responses in children of different temperaments:

The easy child. Look at all the pretty decorations. I'm happy to be here. I like parties. It's fun to play with the other kids. Oh, look! There's my friend. I think I'll check out what he's doing.

The slow-to-warm-up child. There are so many people here! I know some of the kids from my playgroup, but who's that over there? And what about that group of kids in the corner? What are they doing? And who are all these adults? And look at all the decorations. And the music. It's all just too much for me to handle right now! I need some time to get used to this party place and to watch what the others are doing before I feel ready to join in. If I sit on my mommy's lap that will help me to feel more confident.

The challenging child. Ta-da! I'm here! When do we get to eat the cake? What? We're playing pin the tail on the donkey? No, no, no! We must eat the cake first because that's what I want to do. That's my favorite party activity and I've been so looking forward to it since I got up this morning. If I don't get to have it now, I'm going to be very upset!

The active child. Oh, look! Those kids are playing with beach balls. That looks like fun. I think I'll join in. But what's that? Those presents look awfully pretty. I bet I could climb up the whole pile just like a staircase. I wonder what's in that closet? Let me go see! All the grownups are eating things from a tray on top of the counter. If I pull this chair over there, I can have one, too.

Active children love each other's company. They can run around and chase each other with the same amount of boundless energy. You should be watchful however, as the level of activity could escalate to a point where the children become overstimulated, reckless, and could possibly hurt themselves or each other. Riding toys and climbing structures will be particularly enjoyable for active kids.

YOU AND YOUR CHILD
How your temperaments work together

It can be very difficult to understand a child whose style is the complete opposite of your own. On the other hand, there's just as much potential for conflict if you and your child share the same temperament. It's important that you accept and adapt to your child's style and not try to mold her personality. Just as it would be impossible to try to change the color of your child's eyes, trying to change her basic personality is an exercise in futility. The more you understand your child's temperament and how it affects her behavior, the less you are apt to misinterpret her actions. For example, if your challenging child has a tantrum at a social event, she is not doing it to spite you. Likewise, a slow-to-warm-up child who refuses to "kiss Aunt Jackie good-bye" is not deliberately snubbing her aunt or trying to embarrass you.

It's important to avoid communicating—however subtly—any negative attitude you may have about your child's personality. If your child has heard you refer to her as "difficult" or "painfully shy" or "a little tornado" she will behave in such a way that will mirror your attitude toward her. But, if instead you convey the pleasure that you get from your child's personality ("She's really high-spirited" or "She's very careful") you will be rewarded with the most positive aspects of your child's temperament.

The different temperament types may affect your own feelings as a parent in some of the following ways.

You and your easy child

If you're the parent of an easy child, you'll probably find yourself counting your blessings every day. You may find it effortless to integrate your child into everyday activities. Her obliging adaptability means that you don't have to worry about her reactions to new situations or sudden changes in plans. Because your child is so flexible and amenable, your confidence in your parenting abilities will most likely be high.

The danger in having an easy child is that it can be possible to overlook her distress and expect too much of her. Because her reactions tend to be moderate, she may not reveal sadness or anger readily. She may even disguise her feelings because she mistakenly believes that you don't want to see her upset. It's important, therefore, that you be attuned to signals—however subtle—that she is distressed, tired, angry, or in need of comfort. It's also crucial that you encourage her to express her negative emotions and stand up for herself when the need arises.

You and your slow-to-warm-up child

You may be concerned over your child's tentative nature, worried about whether she'll ever become independent or how she will fare in the real world as an adult. If you tend to be on the shy side yourself, you may feel empathetic to your child, allowing her the time she needs to warm up to new situations. Or, you may feel overly protective of your child, wanting to shield her from any distress a new experience might cause. You may even feel secretly grateful that your child's shyness makes it easier for you to bow out of social situations yourself.

If, on the other hand, you're an outgoing person, you may have a difficult time understanding your child's reticence and you may feel frustrated or constricted by her reserve. Some parents feel embarrassed by their child's shy nature and fear how others will perceive their parenting skills.

It's important that you avoid labeling—or allowing others to label—your child as "shy." Though you may have her best intentions at heart as you try to shield her from being pushed into an activity before she's ready, calling her "shy" will affect how she sees herself and may perpetuate her timidity into her adulthood. It may help to keep in mind that your child may be perfectly comfortable with her way of approaching new situations. If others remark on your child's shy nature, you can explain that she takes her time warming up to new situations—and then give her that time.

If your child...	Do say	Don't say
is easy	"What do you think about that?" or "Do you like that?" Engage in conversation so that your child feels comfortable expressing her feelings.	"Nothing ever bothers her. She never gets upset."
is slow to warm up	"Let's look at what those kids are doing and let's decide how you can join them."	"Why don't you play with the others? There's nothing to be afraid of."
is challenging	"I see that you're upset. Let's step away for a second so you can calm down."	"Why must you always be so difficult? You have no reason to get so upset."
is active	"Stay close to me and show me how you can jump."	"Slow down. Be still."

You and your challenging child

Parents of this type of child may find their patience and good intentions consistently frustrated. Because a challenging child makes everything you do so much harder, you may be exhausted and tense much of the time. Even if you're a naturally even-tempered person, you may find yourself yelling often. Parenting a challenging child may cause you to curtail social interactions because of your embarrassment over your child's behavior, which in turn may cause you to feel isolated. If you've experienced others' annoyance or discomfort over your child's intensity, you may feel subtly criticized for not being able to control your child more, and you may find yourself questioning your parenting abilities. If you have other children, you may resent your "high-maintenance" child for draining so much attention away from the others.

In fact, you may feel so emotionally and physically drained that you may find it hard to see the positive attributes of a challenging child or even to enjoy the good times you have with her. When this happens, it's a good idea to remind yourself that your child is not making life difficult for you intentionally; she simply cannot help the way she is. It also helps to remember the fun times you've shared with her in the past and keep in mind that there will be many in the future. Just as your child has intense reactions to the things that distress her, so she has intense reactions to the things that give her pleasure. You may find it helpful to schedule regular time-outs for yourself, to allow yourself some breathing space from your child. Keep in mind, too, that though your child's basic temperament will not change as she grows up, with your guidance her ability to cooperate will grow considerably as she matures.

As difficult as it may be, you will need to learn to stay calm during your child's inevitable outbursts. Trying to make her stop whining or telling her to calm down may only cause her to explode further. Instead, find a room or other place where you can separate her from others who may be disturbed by her reactions so that she can work through her feelings.

Rather than thinking of your child as difficult or stubborn, think of the positive aspects of her personality: persistent, high-spirited, exuberant. Challenging children are often sensitive and demonstrative, and when they express their love, it's most often spontaneous and sincere. Also, because of the force of their personalities, challenging children often become leaders and are less apt to be influenced by their peers. They also tend to be creative and independent thinkers, not content to go along with the crowd. And as your child becomes more independent she will discover how to channel her passion and find better ways of handling frustration. Finally, it can be comforting to know that many challenging children become exceptional, highly accomplished adults.

You and your active child

If you yourself are active, you'll particularly delight in your child's ability to (almost) keep up with you. You'll enjoy special times together, perhaps at an earlier age than other parent-child teams.

If you are a more laid-back type, however, your active child may be downright exhausting, and you may be tempted to view her activity level as a direct challenge to your authority. To keep the positive aspects of your relationship intact, while not trying to keep up with your child's activity level, consider enlisting others' help in joining your child's activities. Enroll her in a morning nursery school program that concentrates on lots of movement. Invest in an age-appropriate at-home climber so that your child can satisfy her need to move without your having to get down on the floor with her for more climbing and rolling around than you really want.

HELPING YOUR CHILD GROW
Working with your child's personality

Understanding and accepting your child's personality does not mean that you should allow her to act any way her temperament dictates. If your child is to succeed socially in life, she needs you to help her modify those natural tendencies that do not serve either

her or her environment. In fact, it's your duty to help your child learn to offset the difficulties of her temperament. Following are some suggestions for helping your child make the most of her positive qualities while tempering those that are less desirable.

The easy child

Most of an easy child's traits are delightful. Where your child will need help is in learning to speak up for herself and not allowing others to take advantage of her agreeable nature.

Teach your child to use words when she needs something. Because easy children tend not to be as demanding as other two-year-olds, they may not express their needs. Take advantage of opportunities as they arise. If your child has been playing at the playground and she appears to be tiring, you can ask her, "Are you feeling tired?" If she answers yes, ask her, "Would you like to go home now?" If she answers yes again, you then might say, "It's okay to tell Daddy if you're tired and want to go home. The next time you feel tired, just tell me."

Encourage your child to be assertive. Easy children may not fight for their rights with other kids. It's a good idea to address situations as they arise. If another child has swiped your child's doll, for instance, you can tell her, "You can say, 'That's my doll.'"

The slow-to-warm-up child

While you should avoid trying to force your child to become more outgoing, you can help her to become more confident in new situations and practice her social skills.

Avoid labeling your child. Calling your child "shy," even if you mean well, will affect how she views herself. It may even provide her with an excuse as she gets older for getting out of situations that make her feel uncomfortable.

Prepare your child for social activities. Joining a group will be easier for your child if she knows what to expect ahead of time. You might tell her who will be there and what will happen. If it's a place she has been to before or there are people there that she has previously met, you might recall any pleasant memories of past events. For instance, you might say, "We're going to visit my friend Irene and her daughter Maria. Do you remember the last time we were there and you played with Maria's special doll collection? I remember how much you said you liked playing with her dolls."

Don't force your child to interact. Slow-to-warm-up children can be overwhelmed by a large group. Don't force your child to join in a group activity. Instead, be encouraging, and let her join in at her own pace.

Reassure your child. Let your child know that it's okay to stay on the sidelines until she's ready to join in. Assure her, too, that she will eventually feel like playing with the others.

Gently prod your child. You want to be careful that you don't give in to your child's reticence at the expense of her learning to interact with others. After she's has had some time to get comfortable with a new situation, gently urge her to forge ahead and join in the activity.

Think small. A large playgroup may be overwhelming for your child. Consider forming or finding a playgroup with just a few children. Also, try to include younger children; they may help your child feel more comfortable and in control.

The challenging child

The challenge for you as a parent of a challenging child is to understand her intense reactions and allow her to express them, while helping her learn what's acceptable and what's not.

Find ways to help your child regain control. Commands and threats usually have no effect on a challenging child when she's in the middle of a tantrum. Instead of struggling with her or responding with equal intensity, help her to calm herself down. A child who is spiraling out of control simply doesn't know how to stop herself. Try saying, "I'm going to help you calm down." This avoids getting into a power struggle and shows her that you're on her side and in control yourself.

You might also consider setting up an "angry corner," where she can take out her frustration on a punching toy. Another method that works for some children is to whisper softly in their ears. This will force a child to quiet down to hear you. Other children respond to being held tightly and lovingly.

Set clear and consistent guidelines for acceptable behavior. Just because your child's reactions are intense, that doesn't mean she should be allowed to express her feelings however she chooses. She needs to learn that she cannot hurt others because she's angry. She's now old enough to learn that her shrieks and screams can be disturbing to others and that there are some places where it's simply not appropriate to have a tantrum. Help her learn that when she begins to feel particularly upset, she must remove herself from the situation until she feels calmer.

Break down transitions into smaller steps. Because they have high persistence, challenging children often have trouble stopping an activity they're engaged in to do something else. Telling your child to stop playing with a toy because it's time for bed may send her into a prolonged tantrum that may get her so emotionally wound up that she may not be able to fall asleep for hours. A better response than simply commanding your child to stop an activity would be to gradually work up to it in small increments.

For instance, you might have her change into her pajamas earlier in the evening. Then you might have her brush her teeth. Let her take along a piece of whatever she's playing with so she doesn't feel like she has to stop what she's doing altogether. Finally, use a pleasurable ritual, such as reading to her, as the final transition before going to bed. You might start off reading to her in the same location where she's playing with the toy and then finish the second half when she's in her bed.

Praise her efforts at cooperation. Acting with restraint doesn't come easily for challenging children. So it's important that you acknowledge when she does try to rein in her behavior and praise her: "Thank you for getting dressed without a fuss. I know you really didn't feel like going out"; "You must be very proud of how you handled your anger at your friend."

Anticipate problem areas and let your child know what you expect of her. Suppose you're planning a long car trip and from past experience you know your child will make a fuss and even wriggle herself out of her seat belt. Before you get in the car, tell your child where you are going, and how long it will take. Since a two-year-old does not yet have a clear concept of time, you'll need to explain to her in terms she can understand. Say, "We're going to Grandma's. We should be there by lunchtime. You'll be sitting in the back seat with your seat belt on. If you feel restless, you can ask us to stop for a break." It's also a good idea to remind your child of any pleasant memories she had on her last trip so she has something to look forward to.

Allow your child leeway in some areas. Maybe your child likes to sing at the top of her lungs in the morning. Maybe you like to have your quiet. But allowing her to exercise something that gives her pleasure may help avoid some power struggles in other areas.

If she starts to sing loudly in a restaurant, for instance, you can say, "I know how much you like to sing. But restaurants are not the place for singing. You can do that at home." And she knows that she can because you've allowed her to in the past.

The active child

Much of your energy will be taken up with keeping your active child safe. To help her adapt to times when she needs to be less active:

Make sure your child has had her nap and has had something nutritious to eat before attending an event. A tired or hungry child will be more apt to get overstimulated, making it harder for her to sit still for any length of time.

Let your child exercise before going anyplace where she has to sit quietly. Shopping trips, restaurants, religious worship, and social affairs can be tough on active children who are expected to sit quietly. To make it easier on your child, build in some time before you have to be where you're going to allow your child to engage in active play.

Work activity into as many routines as possible. When you're running errands, let your child walk instead of putting her in a stroller, which will do nothing toward releasing her natural energy. Use a harness to keep her from wandering (or running) into trouble.

Teach your child some relaxation techniques to calm her down when she begins to get antsy. For instance, you can teach her to breathe deeply 10 times. Or give her a concentration game, such as counting all the people wearing something blue.

Why I act the way I do

Your two-year-old's behavior

Tell people you have a two-year-old and invariably their first response is, "Ah! The terrible twos!" It's a knee-jerk reaction, one that surely captures at least a part of what two-year-olds are like. But labeling twos as terrible is like looking at a construction site through a tiny slit in a barrier wall. You see glimpses of the framework, but it's hard to imagine it as a beautiful, finished building. When you call two-year-olds "terrible," the label gives you an inkling of their behavior without putting it in context, and without letting you see what's so *terrific* about being two.

So what's so great about two-year-olds' behavior? To begin with, this is an age filled with so many firsts: it's the first time your child can be a real companion to you; it's the first time you'll hear your child say, "I love you!"; it's the first time he can play by himself for 15 minutes; it's the first time he shows empathy toward others.

Two-year-olds *adore* their parents, and they're not afraid to shower them with kisses and hugs. You may hear the words "I love you" as often as you hear your two-year-old say "No." At this age, your child sincerely wants to please you, and because he fears the loss of your love more than anything, he will conform to your rules of behavior more easily than an older child would. To experience the world in the company of a two-year-old is to appreciate the beauty, the mystery, and the comedy of life.

So much of your child's behavior at this age is truly wonderful, but misbehavior—because it demands a response—tends to over-shadow the more agreeable behaviors. When we want to chastise someone for behaving badly, we say, "You're acting like a two-year-old." But unlike adults, two-year-olds don't mean to misbehave. They're simply too young to be that devious. And they don't know the rules of proper behavior yet. That has to be taught. Understanding your child's misbehaviors within the context of his development puts a whole new light on why two-year-olds act the way they do.

DEVELOPMENTAL MILESTONE
Anticipating your reactions

Though your two-year-old certainly is not yet capable of making moral judgments or even guessing about whether a certain activity is a good or bad thing to do, he is just beginning to recognize that his behavior—and misbehavior—calls for a response from you.

Who's in charge?

Contrariness is typical for most two-year-olds. No sooner do you get your child dressed than he tears off his clothes. Bedtime means time to escape. Bathtime leads to tears. Nearly any restriction you place on your child's behavior can result in sobbing, screaming, hitting, and "limp-body syndrome." Your child doesn't intend to make your life difficult. But everything is so new and wonderful and fascinating to him, and he wants to explore everything he sees. His wants and needs take center stage, but because he does not always have the ability to say what he wants or feels, and he hasn't yet developed the self-control to regulate his actions, his behavior can be downright disagreeable.

Sometimes it may seem like your child is out to get you to do what he wants—whatever it takes. But two-year-olds are simply too young to understand the concept of true manipulation. What may seem like defiance is merely your child's way of pushing the boundaries of his new sense of independence. He's testing the waters, to see if he can get what he wants. And he's learned that there are many different ways of getting what he wants besides crying and screaming. This is one aspect of cause-and-effect that he seems to grasp quite easily.

Let's say you've finally gotten your child to bed after much coaxing and cajoling. No sooner do you turn out the light than you hear a plaintive request: "Mommy, water?" You bring him the water and are about to leave his room once again, but you're stopped in your tracks when he sweetly calls out, "Mommy, kiss?" As you plant a kiss on his forehead, he says, "More book?" or "Sing." Before you know it, your child has effectively delayed his bedtime another half hour.

Though your child isn't even sure exactly *what* he wants, he does know that these requests keep you in his presence a little while longer. He puts off, for just a little bit, the time when he must separate from you. He simply pulls out those tricks that have worked for him in the past.

Common misbehaviors

Hitting, shoving, biting, kicking, grabbing, throwing things—these are the sorts of behaviors that make parents wince and that two-year-olds naturally engage in. Two-year-olds act aggressively for many reasons. To begin with, their verbal skills are still quite limited. When a child doesn't yet have the ability to say how he feels or what he needs, hitting, shoving, or biting can act as a kind of verbal shorthand. Whacking a playmate who has snatched his toy truck gets the desired result—the child releases the truck. Trying to say, "I'm angry because you took my truck and I want it back," would be nearly impossible for a two-year-old, plus it would not have nearly the desired effect of the whack.

Two-year-olds also haven't learned how to curb their impulses. If your child feels like shoving his baby sister, he just does it. It never enters his mind that this is not socially acceptable behavior and that it might hurt his sister. Face it, adults have the same impulses. Someone cuts in front of you in line or takes the parking space you were just maneuvering into, and you fume. You may feel like punching the line interloper or doing serious damage to the rude driver's car. But you've learned that society has put restrictions on such behavior. Your two-year-old hasn't yet learned about those constraints.

The frustration level for two-year-olds is also extremely high, and this can lead to aggressive behavior. Your child wants what he wants *when* he wants it and the *way* he wants it, and when things don't go his way he becomes frustrated. He may express that frustration through physical acts of aggression.

Dawdling and whining

While it may seem that your child drags his heels just to annoy you, he doesn't see it that way. As far as he's concerned, he's not dawdling at all. Two-year-olds have a different sense of time than do adults. They live for the moment—not for where they have to be in the future. They also don't have a good sense of how long it will take them to accomplish certain tasks, and they may truly believe that they can do two things at once. They're easily distracted. And they simply cannot move at the same pace as you can.

Dawdling may be annoying, but there's probably no other behavior that gets on a parent's nerves quite the way whining does. Almost anything can send a two-year-old into fits of whining: hunger, fatigue, boredom, lack of attention, overstimulation, telling him "No." And often, children know that if they continue this high-pitched torture, they'll wear down their parents enough that eventually a *no* will turn into a *yes*.

How it feels to be me

When your child has a tantrum, it's because he feels as though he has lost control, that his will has been thwarted by the grown-up who has all the power in the relationship. Here's what might be going through your child's mind before he launches into a tantrum:

I want that toy. I want that toy now. But I can't possibly have it unless Mommy buys it. Why won't she buy it for me? Can't she see that I need that toy? I wannit, I wannit, I wannit. I've been so good, trailing along quietly on this boring errand. And now I'm really tired and I want to go home. I deserve a reward. But Mommy's telling me "No." It's always "No" this and "No" that. It's not fair! I'm getting really upset! I don't like the way I'm feeling. It's scary. But I can't help myself. I just feel like screaming.

CONFLICT
Being "good" but not knowing why

Your child is just beginning to learn that certain behaviors, such as hitting, biting, shoving, and grabbing another child's toys, are not acceptable. But he does not yet fully understand why. So one time when a playmate snatches his toy, he may express his anger properly through words, or maybe tears. But the next time, he may bite his playmate. When you scold him or punish him for his actions, he may not understand that what he did was wrong. He'll apologize if you make him, but he won't necessarily feel any remorse.

The reason for such inconsistency is that two-year-olds have not yet developed a conscience—that inner voice that tells us something is right or wrong based on how it will make the other person feel. Two-year-olds are still enormously egocentric. Because their world revolves around their own needs and desires, they do not understand that their actions can hurt others. Plus, they do not have enough experience to comprehend the cause-and-effect of their actions. They simply do not grasp that biting or hitting someone might hurt the person. When they get bitten or hit enough by their playmates or siblings, they'll learn that biting and hitting might hurt the other person. They also learn when they begin to develop empathy, which you can help teach them by saying things like, "When you hit Josh it hurts him." The way to teach your child not to bite or hit is not by doing the same thing to him in return. Be firm but gentle when you discipline your child.

YOU AND YOUR CHILD
Determining what's important

Understanding what behaviors are normal for two-year-olds can help lessen your own frustration with your child's conduct and improve your interaction with him. Tugging your arm in a supermarket, toileting lapses, not eating everything that's on his plate, and spilling a glass of milk are not behaviors that warrant disciplinary measures. To the contrary, these are all actions that signify your child's struggles with his stage of development. He tugs your arm because he needs your attention at that moment; he has a toileting lapse because he has not yet developed the physical coordination to make it to the potty in time (see Chapter 10); he leaves his food on the plate because he feels full; he spills the milk because he does not have the motor skills to grasp a cup firmly every time. Before you consider disciplining your child, ask yourself whether his behavior is something he can control. Hitting another child is something he can learn not to do; waking you in the middle of the night because he's scared of monsters is not something over which he has any restraint.

When you do discipline your child, the manner in which you approach the task makes an enormous difference in how your child will relate to you and in how well your message will come across. Above all, maintain a tone of compassion when you correct your child's behavior. You want your child to feel secure, to know that even if he did something to displease you, you still love him. His behavior may have been bad, but *he* is not bad. When your child feels secure in your love, he'll be willing to accept the limits you impose because he wants, above all, to please you.

The way you approach discipline will also influence how your child relates to others. For example, scolding him loudly and doling out harsh punishments will frighten him into obedience. But the ultimate effect of such approaches will be that your child develops a conscience that kicks in only because he fears the consequences, not because he genuinely cares about others' feelings or doing what's right for its own sake.

Hitting or spanking a child may get him to stop the misbehavior for a time, but it teaches him that physical aggression is an acceptable response if you don't like what another person is doing. And because you are much larger than your child, you are teaching him that it's okay to hit someone who is smaller or weaker than you are. Your child will likely take these lessons out into the world, solving conflicts physically rather than by more constrained means.

Being overly permissive with your child can also backfire, making it difficult for your child to gain maturity and self-discipline. He may have trouble following rules, and may grow up feeling unsure of what is expected of him or how to interact with others.

The best approach to discipline, called "authoritative" by many experts, lies somewhere between the two extremes. By clearly laying out rules, firmly and consistently enforcing them, and by letting your child know that you expect him to behave in a certain way, while encouraging his independence and individuality, you help your child feel secure. This, in turn, will help him to grow into a self-assured, self-disciplined adult.

When you address your child's misbehavior, how you express your anger can make the a big difference between humiliating your child or helping him to understand that his behavior is not acceptable.

If your child...	Do say	Don't say
hits a playmate who snatched his toy	"I know you're mad that Adam took your toy. But you're not allowed to hit. It hurts Adam."	"That's a bad boy!"
continues to play with a puzzle after you've told him it's time to go to bed	"I don't like it when you don't listen to me. I need you to go to bed now."	"Don't you *dare* ignore me!"
whines and tugs at you when you stop to talk to a friend	"I know waiting can be hard, but that's your job right now."	"Stop being such a brat!"
draws on the wall after being reminded to draw only on paper	"Drawing on the wall is not allowed. Help me clean this and then we'll put your crayons away for another day."	"Now look what you've done! You never listen."

Handling your own anger

It's inevitable that your child's misbehavior will anger—even enrage—you. When that happens, you may feel yourself spiraling out of control. Your throat constricts, blood rushes to your face, and you start yelling—maybe even screaming—at your child. Your child's feelings are far from your mind, and you may even have forgotten what exactly made you so angry in the first place. When these kinds of outbursts occur on a regular basis, it can be destructive, not only to your child, but to your ability to discipline.

When your anger is out of control, your capacity to discipline effectively is also diminished. Your child now experiences you as unpredictable. He may feel threatened by your anger and may simply give up trying to please you.

If you have a loving relationship with your child, and he feels secure in your love for him, then losing your temper on occasion is not as damaging as it is in a home where the child does not have a secure relationship with his parent. However, it's not a good idea to swallow your anger or pretend that your child has done absolutely nothing wrong. Anger is a healthy human emotion, and your child needs to know if he has done something that warrants your disapproval. The key is not to allow your anger to control you, but rather to express your anger calmly. You'll find that your two-year-old will listen to what you have to say much more readily than if you simply scream at him.

Even if you do find your anger spinning out of control on occasion, you can act to repair the damage. First, get down to your child's level and acknowledge that you said some hurtful things. Then tell your child that you were upset and that's not how you really think of him. Calmly explain what he did to make you angry and how you intend to handle his misbehavior in the future. Be sure to give him plenty of hugs and kisses.

To avoid future blowups, try to determine what behaviors in your child trigger intense anger in you. It might be your child's dawdling when you're trying to get to work. Or perhaps it's that he continues to play when you've told him it's time to stop. At these moments you might hear yourself say, "He's lazy," or "He's ignoring me." These are your trigger thoughts. The next step is to reframe these thoughts by stopping for a moment and considering what's really going on. Ask yourself why your child might be behaving that way, keeping in mind that your child doesn't *want* to make you angry. In fact, he wants you to be pleased with him. Once you've formed an explanation (for instance, "My child has a hard time concentrating in the morning"), you'll better be able to address the situation in a calm, constructive manner.

HELPING YOUR CHILD GROW
Disciplining effectively

Good discipline means much more than correcting your child's misbehavior. Your main objective is to encourage your child to behave in positive ways and become a cooperative family member. The more you set the stage for good behavior, the less time you'll spend correcting your child's misbehavior.

Establishing routines

Besides making *your* life easier, routines and schedules create order and predictability in your child's world. Knowing what to expect and when allows him to gain a sense of control over his environment. In turn, he will cooperate more and balk less when it's time to stop playing to eat dinner or go to bed. When your child knows, for instance, that after he has breakfast, he gets dressed, goes for a walk to the park where he can play, and then home for a nap, he has an easier time preparing himself for what will happen next. It's when children don't know what to expect that they become confused, which leads to whining, demanding, and throwing tantrums. And when your daily routines take into consideration your child's desires as well as your needs, your child will be more apt to follow them without much fuss. Certain times of day or situations lend themselves to establishing routines.

At mealtime. Try to schedule breakfast, lunch, and dinner at around the same time each day. Give your child simple tasks that he can perform as part of the mealtime routine, such as placing napkins by each plate or carrying a lightweight dish to the table. If possible, try to have the whole family together during dinner. Besides making this a routine, this practice will give your child some consistent time with other family members. You can also put some routine into cleanup by giving your child one or two simple tasks, such as handing you his plate while you're at the sink, or helping sort washed utensils.

At bedtime. When your child knows that every night after dinner he brushes his teeth, takes a bath, listens to one story, sings a song, and says goodnight to all his stuffed animals, it makes the transition from awake time to sleep time much easier. He can prepare himself and look forward to each activity because he knows, for instance, that storytime always follows bathtime.

If your child's nighttime routine has been to fall asleep while watching TV, or in your bed, you may have a more difficult time undoing these bad habits as your child resists the new routine. Be patient and consistent; eventually your child will learn to adjust.

At playtime. Getting a two-year-old to clean up toys can seem as impossible as asking a horse to fly. The last thing your child wants to do is clean up his toys after you've made him stop playing with them. Or, if he stopped playing to move on to something else, the toys are ancient history as far as he's concerned. But you can get your child to make small strides. Instead of issuing general commands, such as "Clean up your room," break the task down into small, manageable steps that are followed in the same order each time. To begin, ask your child to help while showing him what to do. You might say, "Would you help me put the puzzle pieces back in the box?" As you start to put the pieces away, chances are your child will join in the activity. Gradually, increase his responsibility so that he is eventually doing most of the putting away. You can sweeten the deal by making an enjoyable activity, such as reading a story together, part of the cleanup routine. If your child has something to look forward to after the chore, he'll be more willing to cooperate.

If your child refuses to help you put away the toys, don't get into a battle with him. Wait a few minutes, then try again. If you find this happening repeatedly, it could be that your timing is off. Perhaps your child needs a little cooling off time after play before he's ready to launch into a cleanup. Or maybe you need to end the play session with a less stimulating activity.

In the car. Whether you're making a quick trip to the store to pick up groceries or are planning a long drive, you can make the time in your car pleasant for both of you by following a basic set of rituals. To begin, always put your child in a car seat with restraints. If you have a cassette player, you might play some of his favorite songs. Or you can recite some fun rhymes. Small toys within your child's reach also make good company. You can help your child pass the time by playing travel games, such as pointing out cars of a particular color, or looking for certain signs or numbers. If you're planning a longer trip, make sure to stop at least every two hours for a bathroom and possibly snack break. When your child knows to expect stops, he'll be better able to handle the confinement.

Choosing your battles

Trying to get your child to abide by every rule can be exhausting and aggravating, both for you and your child. In trying to direct every aspect of your child's behavior, you could be setting yourself up for constant battles as your child tries to assert his newfound independence. If you're willing to ease up a bit on some things, you'll find that your child will become more cooperative in other areas. The key is knowing which rules you're willing to bend a little and which ones are nonnegotiable. Those that are hard and fast usually concern safety, health, and values, such as holding an adult's hand while crossing the street, wearing a hat and mittens in cold weather, and being considerate of others. You can be more flexible with those that revolve around your child's preferences, as well as convenience. Allowing your child to watch a half hour more of TV than normal for a special program, wear clothes that don't match, or eat normally forbidden cookies when visiting a relative are examples of the kind of flexibility that won't do your child any harm and may make him more willing to conform to other rules. Likewise, honoring your child's preferences on a regular basis, when they don't involve breaking the rules, will also make it easier for your child to do what's expected of him.

Once you've decided which rules you'll be flexible with and which ones are nonnegotiable, stick by them. Avoid having too many regulations, though, because it will be difficult for your child to remember and follow them.

The best way to get your child to follow the guidelines you set for him is to remind him what you expect beforehand, rather than waiting for him to misbehave. For instance, before a trip to the grocery store, you can tell your child that he can pick out one treat for himself, but no more. Be sure to tell him if certain treats are off-limits. Ignore any requests for more treats. Or, as it nears his bedtime, review the nightly routine as a way of reinforcing your rules. Finally, make sure your child not only knows the rules, but the consequences of breaking them. Then follow through with the punishment if he misbehaves.

Catching your child being good
It's so easy to notice and correct the misbehaviors your child engages in. But catching him when he's behaving admirably—and praising him for what he did right—is just as important, if not more so. When your child shares a treasured toy with a playmate or asks politely for something he wants, make sure you let him know that you noticed and that you're proud of the way he

behaved. The good feeling he gets when you praise him for behaving well will encourage him to repeat the behavior.

Catching your child being good can work particularly well for those areas that tend to be troublesome. Let's say your child interrupts you, demanding attention whenever you're on the phone. As soon as the phone rings, remind him that he needs to be quiet while you're on the phone. After about 30 seconds—before he starts to grow impatient—thank him for being quiet. If he interrupts a couple of minutes later, thank him for waiting so long before interrupting. The positive attention you give him for being patient will help him the next time around.

Fostering patience and delaying gratification

Many behavioral issues arise out of a two-year-old's need to have what he wants *when* he wants it. Learning to be patient and to delay gratification will help your child be cooperative in a number of areas. A child who has learned these skills won't be as likely to interrupt your phone conversations looking for attention; he will be less apt to throw a tantrum over not being allowed a cookie before dinner if he knows he'll get one after dinner; and he will be more cooperative in performing unpleasant tasks, such as picking up his toys, if he has learned that the payoff is getting some snuggle time with you as you read him a story.

Age two is not too young to teach your child to wait. However, keep in mind that he can't be expected to wait patiently for more than 30 seconds. If you are able to do something in a moment, tell your child and then follow through. Make sure that his patience is rewarded. Say, "Thank you for waiting. I know it's hard to do." This way he'll feel good about waiting, not view it as some terrible chore.

Admittedly, these are enormously difficult skills to teach a two-year-old. One of the best ways is through example. When you keep your promises to your child, he'll be more cooperative because he knows that if he's patient, his needs will be met. Showing your child how patience can pay off will also help him learn the value of waiting. Let him know when you're pleased with yourself for having worked hard at completing a job to your satisfaction. Be sure to praise him when he does the same. ("You put away all your blocks! I'm really proud of you!")

Limiting misbehavior

Teaching your child to cooperate is a worthy goal, but no two-year-old will behave properly all the time. In fact, it's natural for your child to test the limits to see how much he can get away with. Your goal is to limit those behaviors you don't want, while allowing your child enough latitude to make mistakes and learn from them.

Dealing with dawdling

To avoid the friction that your child's dawdling inevitably causes, you need to make changes in how *you* approach situations, rather than forcing your child to change.

Identify which times your child is most likely to dawdle. Getting ready in the morning and going to bed at night are two times that seem to exacerbate dawdling. Build in time to include your child's dawdling in your routine. For instance, if mornings are a problem, prepare as much as you can the night before and wake up a little earlier. If your child becomes pokey before bedtime, start his nightly routine early enough so that he can get to bed on time without you having to push him.

Give yourself more time to accomplish tasks. If you're running errands with your child in tow, expect that he will not be able to comb store aisles as quickly as you and that he will most likely get distracted. If you've given yourself a schedule that's too tight, you'll find yourself nagging your child to keep pace. Likewise, try not to schedule activities for your child too close together. He'll need enough time to make the transition from one to another.

Try to determine why your child is dawdling. Sometimes children dawdle because they feel anxious. For instance, your child may be prolonging the time when he has to leave in the morning because he doesn't want to separate from you. Other times, your child may simply be too absorbed in an activity to stop. Because he does not yet have a grasp of time, he may actually believe that he can finish his activity and be ready to go out the door with you simultaneously.

Find creative ways to get your child to move more quickly. Putting on a lively music tape in the morning, for instance, may help him get ready faster. You might even challenge him to finish a task before a certain song has finished playing. You could also use a timer to make a game out of getting ready. Just be sure that you give him plenty of time to complete his task so that he can feel successful.

Build in lots of time for TLC. Waking your child with a big hug and a kiss instead of a command to hurry up and get ready will go a long way in helping him be more cooperative.

Preventing whining

While it may be tempting to give in to your child to stop his whining, the danger is that if you give in, he will learn that it's an effective tool to get what he wants. Here are some better ways to halt the whining:

Identify the "why" behind the whine. Is your child hungry, tired, lonely, bored, frustrated? Asking a two-year-old what's bothering him, though, isn't likely to work. Even if your child knows, he probably can't articulate it in words. Instead, ask your child specific questions, such as, "Are you tired?" "Are you hungry?" Then, try to resolve the problem.

State the rules on whining. A good time to do this is before your child has become upset. Let him know that he will not get what he wants by whining. Explain that when he whines you can't understand him. But if he asks for something in a polite way, using his "regular voice," you will consider his request. Then make sure you follow your own policy.

Use humor. Instead of getting angry at your child, find a way to turn his whining into laughter. You might ask if you can join in with his whining. See who's the best whiner. Or you could go on a "whine hunt," pretending not to know where the whine is coming from. Injecting a note of silliness—without mocking your child— can help deflate the whining while at the same time teach your child that whining won't get him anywhere.

Ignore the whining. When all else fails, simply pretend you don't hear your child. Avoid making eye contact, don't respond verbally, and act calmly and neutrally, even if you feel angry. Admittedly, this is harder to do than it sounds, but your child will soon stop when he sees his whines have no effect.

Praise your child for not whining. When your child asks for something in an appropriate way, be sure to point out to him what he did right. Then consider his request and, if appropriate, give him what he wants.

Ending bedtime battles

If your child balks at bedtime, it could be for a number of reasons: he could be afraid of the dark or of separating from you; his habits have taught him to associate sleep with other activities, such as watching the TV; he doesn't want to miss out on anything that's going on around him; or his regular schedule is disrupted. In addition to establishing a nightly "goodnight" routine, here are some suggestions for helping bedtime go more smoothly:

Help cut down on your child's fears. If he's afraid of the dark, put a night-light on in his room or keep his door ajar with the hall light filtering in until he's sound asleep. If he fears being separated from you, be sure you give him plenty of attention and affection during the day. You might also consider providing your child with a security object to help him separate from you more easily. *(For more on nighttime fears, see Chapter 7.)*

Don't pique your child's curiosity. Some children simply don't want to miss out on anything. They will resist any attempt to put them to bed while you're having a good time. While you're getting your child ready for bed, keep the lights in the living areas turned low, keep the volume of the TV or stereo turned down, and keep your "grown-up" plans to yourself.

Stick to your routines. Your child needs to understand that bedtime follows a predictable daily pattern. If the routine changes every night, he'll readily look for ways to extend his day.

Taming tantrums

Sooner or later, no matter how well-behaved your child is, he will erupt in a temper tantrum. Some children seem to fly into a rage at the drop of a hat. Others go into meltdown only when they feel pushed to the extreme. Witnessing your child face down on the floor, kicking, screaming, and possibly holding his breath, can be disturbing and frightening, not to mention embarrassing if it happens in a public place.

Although you can't prevent tantrums altogether, you can cut down the number of episodes and help your child regain control. You want to avoid priming your child for a tantrum in the first place. Be alert for signs that he might be becoming overly frustrated, anxious, hungry, or tired. Then do what you can to head off a tantrum before it starts. You may also want to review the limits you've put on your child. Are they too severe? Have you allowed your child any latitude or choices? Do you find yourself saying "No" to nearly all of your child's requests? Realizing what sets off your child and avoiding those situations when possible will reduce the number of unpleasant tantrums.

When your child does have a tantrum, here are a few suggestions for helping him regain control:

Take a deep breath and remain calm. This is easier said than done, especially if your child is having a meltdown in your local supermarket. Remember, when a child is having a tantrum, he feels completely out of control. If he senses that you, at least, are in control, he will have an easier time calming down. Yelling at him will only make things worse.

Acknowledge your child's feelings. Say, "I know you're upset. It makes you angry that you can't have that candy bar [or whatever is making your child upset]." Sometimes your child just needs to know that you understand what he's going through.

Don't give in. Giving in to a child's demands will only set a bad precedent, and he'll learn that if he makes a big enough fuss he'll get what he wants. If the tantrum has occurred in a public place, it's better to cut your outing short and take your child home rather than give him what he wants simply to keep the peace. Use words to let your child know that his tantrum won't work: "You will not get what you want by crying and kicking. When you calm down, we'll talk about the problem." Then create a calming-down time, either by offering your child a hug or taking him to a special time-out place.

Once your child has calmed down, you can offer to help him with the thing that was frustrating him, such as helping him to put on his shoes or put a puzzle together.

SAFETY FIRST

Protecting yourself and your child during a tantrum

When a child is wildly out of control, thrashing and kicking, he can be a danger both to himself and to anyone in his path. Here's what you should do to prevent either of you from getting hurt:

• Move your child away from any area that may pose a danger, such as a store display that could fall over if kicked or a piece of furniture with a sharp corner.

• Hold your child from behind by enclosing him in a sturdy but loving grip. Hold him hard enough that you keep his arms from flailing, but not so hard that it frightens him. This lets your child know that you're in control, even if he is not. It also tells him that you will not let him hurt himself or anyone else.

• Speak to your child in soothing tones until he calms down.

Curbing aggressive behavior

Aggressive behavior is normal for two-year-olds. But that doesn't mean you should allow it. Your child needs to know that certain behaviors, such as biting, kicking, hitting, shoving, and throwing things, are not acceptable.

Give your child the right words. Help your child express his anger, frustration, or needs by showing him how he can use words to work through a problem. First, acknowledge (and help him name) his feelings: "You must be very angry right now." Then state the rules very clearly: "You're not allowed to bite. It hurts Jason."

Provide your child with outlets for his frustration and anger. Show your child other more acceptable outlets for his anger, rather than aggression toward another person. Such activities as pounding clay, banging a pot, punching a pillow, and running are all safe ways for your child to release steam.

Don't give your child attention when he acts aggressively.
Your child may have learned that bad behavior will get him more attention than good behavior. Though you do need to step in and stop him from his aggressive behavior, don't overreact or give him any more attention than the moment warrants. Be sure to give him plenty of recognition and praise when he's calm and acting cooperatively. He will soon learn that he doesn't need to throw his cereal bowl or shove his baby sister to get your attention.

Be aware of aggression triggers for your child. An overtired two-year-old can behave irrationally, swinging his fists at a playmate for no reason at all. Determine what times of the day your child tends to get overtired and avoid scheduling playdates or other activities that may cause problems. During these times, watch your child closely for signals that he may be headed for some aggression.

Watch how you play with and discipline your child. Roughhousing can encourage some children to carry that play behavior into everyday behavior. And some children simply do not know where to draw the line between harmless wrestling and hurting another person. Make sure your child understands that hurting other people is not funny and is not allowed—under any circumstances.

Be sure that you're not inadvertently teaching your child to act aggressively through your discipline technique. Biting him back if he bites you or smacking him when he hits a playmate sends him the message that aggression is a perfectly valid response to being upset or angry. Be firm, but gentle, when you're disciplining your child or when he makes you angry.

My fears and nightmares

What makes your two-year-old afraid

Infants and young toddlers are mostly limited to two fears: fear of being separated from their parents and fear of strangers. They may also be afraid of concrete things that directly threaten their sense of safety, such as a crashing boom of thunder or a growling dog. But when a child turns two, her fears can magnify tenfold. She becomes afraid of both the real and the imagined, the rational and the ridiculous, the concrete and the abstract. Her fears may come seemingly out of nowhere and just as mysteriously disappear.

As absurd as it may sound, your child's fears are cause for celebration. The development of fear means she is developing a fertile imagination, knowledge of the world, the ability to think abstractly, greater independence, and a sharp memory. Ironically, all this growth may, in itself, stimulate fears. For instance, because her imagination allows her to pretend that her teddy bears are talking, playing, and drinking tea, she can also conjure up horrible images of monsters and witches who kidnap children. While she knows that the bathtub water goes down the drain, she may deduce that *she* could go down the drain as well. This is a clear example of her ability to grasp the concept of cause and effect without being able to possess the experience to separate what's reasonable and what's preposterous.

DEVELOPMENTAL MILESTONE
Understanding and imagination

As she begins to form a separate identity from her parents, your child becomes aware of her own small size and the dangers lurking in the world, such as stoves that can burn and dogs that can bite. Also, because of her increased mobility, she comes in contact with many more perceived dangers than when she was a baby sheltered in the safety of your arms. She can remember things better than she could when she was younger, such as the time the neighbor's cat scratched her. If the incident was sufficiently frightening, she's likely to remember it the next time a cat approaches her, and she may recoil in fear. Learning new skills can also provoke fears. Two-year-olds tend to be leery of new things until those things have proved themselves harmless. The local pool, in which you try to teach her to swim, may be overwhelming in its size, and your child may feel as though she's going to be swallowed up by it—until experience proves otherwise.

Even the most benign things hold the potential for scaring your two-year-old: vacuum cleaners, sirens, toilets, clowns, lawn mowers, waves, men with mustaches, fairy tales, even Santa

Claus. And while some fears are perfectly rational and help protect your child, such as the fear of running into traffic or the fear of going off with a stranger, other fears seem to have no bearing in either experience or reality. What's more, your child does not yet have the ability to separate the realistic from the fantastic. A monster she imagines under the bed may be just as real and scary as the traffic zooming down a busy boulevard.

Your two-year-old's egocentricity and suggestibility can also play a part in fears. Because she naturally sees herself as the center of the universe, she can easily (and without conscious thought) put herself in the place of characters or other children who are threatened or frightened. Hearing the story of Jack and the Beanstalk, for instance, your child may think to herself, "If Jack can be chased by the giant, so can I!" If a character in a TV show can be bitten by a dog, she can be, too. If a playmate is afraid of the slide at the local playground, your child may also develop that fear simply out of empathy. And if you show anxiety in certain situations, such as crossing a busy street, your child may become fearful right along with you.

Where do fears come from?

Sometimes it's easy to see the origins of your child's fears. Suppose you take her to see a dinosaur exhibit at a natural history museum. Imagine gazing up at a replica of a huge tyrannosaurus—the gaping mouth and fierce fangs, the enormous claws, the scaly skin! If anything is the stuff of terror, surely this is it! If after your visit, your child begins to complain of monsters under her bed, it doesn't take a rocket scientist to figure out how *that* fear developed.

But not all fears are this easy to decipher. For instance, you may take your water-loving child for the first dip of the season at the local lake you've frequented in the past only to find that in the intervening months your child has developed a decided revulsion to the water. She won't even go near it. You rack your brain trying to remember if anything happened last year that could have caused this fear, and come up with nothing. If you ask your child why she's so scared of the water, she won't be able to help you, either. Besides not having the ability to articulate the whys of her fears, she may simply not be able to come up with any explanation. And just as inexplicably as her fear of the water appeared, it may disappear, and your daughter will enthusiastically splash around in the water again.

Most often, fears of fantastical creatures, such as monsters, dragons, or witches tend to appear at night, after your child has gone to bed. Such fears may be a manifestation of your child's separation anxiety. Reluctant to relinquish the safety and comfort of being with you, her mind conjures up the horrors that might await a child alone and unprotected in her bed, in the dark.

The nature of nightmares

Your child's first nightmares may have begun last year; more commonly they begin to occur between the ages of two and three. Again, having a nightmare is a milestone in her development. At this age, your child's mind bursts forth with highly imaginative, though not quite logical, thinking. She also has the growing ability to create pictures in her mind of the world around her. It's during this phase that your child will begin to experience frightening dreams or fears that interrupt her sleep. And because the line between reality and fantasy is still fuzzy for two-year-olds, your child's nightmares may seem absolutely real to her.

A two-year-old's nightmares may consist of either hazy images that generate a sense of terror or intensely vivid scenes of grotesque giants or witches or characters from favorite TV shows. Even lovable and benign creatures, such as Barney or Elmo, may turn into terrifying presences in your child's dreams. Her dreams may be scary enough to wake her, and she may cry out in panic or run to your bedside for comfort.

How much fear is too much?

If your child is having chronic nightmares or if her fears are growing more extreme or more frequent, it may be a signal that she is experiencing some stress or anxiety in her life. You won't always be easily able to pinpoint the source of your child's fears or nightmares, though. Sometimes a child's fear may be completely disconnected from the event that caused it. For instance, if you're returning to work, your child may develop an intense fear of dogs.

Ask yourself the following questions to try to determine if your child's fears may be related to something going on in her life:

- Have there been any major changes going on in my family, such as my spouse or myself returning to work, moving to a new home, the birth of sibling, or a change in caregivers? Because new situations lead to so many unknowns, a child's imagination can run rampant with possibilities. (Does the new baby mean my parents will get rid of me?)
- Have I provided my child with enough structure? Rules, routines, and limits give two-year-olds a sense of security; without them, your child may feel vulnerable.
- Am I expecting too much of my child? A day that's crowded with activities and demands can cause your child to feel stressed.
- Am I communicating my own fears? Children easily pick up on their parents' feelings. How do my own anxieties about my child's well-being or safety manifest themselves in my interactions with her? Are concerns about health, work, or family problems taking their toll on me—and my child?
- Is my child having difficulties with any of the children in day care or her playgroup? If so, your child may have anxieties over returning to the place where she's experiencing problems.

If you can't determine the source of your child's fears and have not been able to alleviate them, you should consult your pediatrician, who may refer you to a therapist.

Understanding fear

The polar bear at the zoo, the dangling spider, the dust bunnies under the bed, the washing machine, the sanitation truck, the swirling water whooshing down the toilet bowl, the storybook witch—all have the potential to frighten a two-year-old. Whatever rationale goes through your child's mind to create her fear, she may quickly forget it. Yet she'll still experience terror at being confronted with the object of her fear, or even the possibility of its manifestation, such as in the case of imaginary ogres.

In fact, your child's emotional reaction, which can quickly veer out of control, can actually be more frightening to her than the source of her original fear. When your child was younger and cried hysterically because she was frightened over something, she didn't have enough self-awareness to understand what was happening. Now that your child is older, she *knows* that she's scared and she *knows* what's causing her fright, and whatever you say isn't necessarily going to make her feel better at that moment. At the same time, your child doesn't have enough emotional experience or resources to say to herself, "I've been scared before and I've gotten over it." All she knows is that she's feeling out of control; that in itself is frightening to her.

If these feelings occur again and again when your child is confronted with a source of fear, instead of accepting the strange thing and coming to terms with whatever it is about the thing that induces fear, your child may end up focusing on the fear itself until it becomes a phobia. A phobia is a persistent, illogical fear of something. Far from being a rare occurrence, more than half of all children between the ages of two and three develop at least one phobia. And it's their developing imaginations that feed these persistent fears.

One of the most common phobias of two-year-olds is brought on by dogs. Let's say that a neighbor is walking his very large rottweiler and the dog lunges at your child. She may be afraid of that dog every time she sees it. But then her imagination kicks in and when she sees a cocker spaniel, she is terrified of that dog, too. This fear of dogs may escalate so that if she so much as sees a dog in the distance, or hears one barking, she becomes afraid. She may even fear looking at pictures of dogs, or fret that a dog is going to come into her room at night and attack her.

How it feels to be me

One of the most common sources of fright to a two-year-old is clowns. How could such a child-friendly character cause your child to whimper or cower with fear? you may wonder. Try seeing a clown from a two-year-old's perspective:

I went to a birthday party and there was a clown there. His hair was all different colors and he had huge feet and this big, round red nose and lots of white around his eyes and a really gigantic mouth. And he talked in this strange voice. I've never seen a person who looked like that or talked like that. I knew he couldn't be a real person like Mommy or Daddy. He was like some kind of a weird human-monster, and that really scared me.

But what scared me even more was that he made some things disappear and other things pop out of nowhere. I never knew what was going to pop up next. And when he got real close to me and looked me in the eye and honked this loud horn, I got really frightened. I wanted to go home right then because who knew what he would do next? Maybe he'd make me disappear or maybe he'd make a witch pop up right next to me.

It's important that you take your child's fears seriously and not try to rationalize them away or make your child feel bad for having them. You can help your child overcome her fears by knowing what to say and what not to say when your child is responding to an immediate fear.

If your child...	Do say	Don't say
screams as you try putting her in the pool with you	"That's okay. We don't have to go in the water right now."	"There's nothing to be afraid of. The water won't hurt you."
refuses to go to bed because she says the monsters will get her	"Let's do something to make sure the monsters stay away." Then go on a make-believe monster hunt.	"There are no such thing as monsters."
cowers behind you when she sees your neighbor walk his dog	Nothing. Allow your child to seek comfort until the dog passes.	"Don't be such a baby. The dog isn't going to bite you."

YOU AND YOUR CHILD
Your feelings about your child's fears

Perhaps your child becomes hysterical when you turn on the vacuum cleaner. Or maybe she runs into your room during the night, claiming that giant bees are circling her bed, and pleading to sleep in your bed. When your child is so obviously distraught, it's natural for you to feel nearly as disturbed as she is. Your heart may go out to her and you want to do whatever it takes to comfort her and assure her that everything will be all right. Or you may wonder if there's something wrong with your child and that may cause you to become frightened yourself. You may even feel embarrassed if her fears are exercised in front of others. It's perfectly normal if you become impatient or exasperated—especially if you can't get your vacuuming done or you've spent night after night coaxing your fearful child back to sleep. Stress, exhaustion from lack of sleep, and anxiety are also common in parents when their kids are experiencing fears. You may even feel anger and think your child is trying to manipulate you.

Though it may be tempting to dismiss your child's fears, it's important that you take them seriously. No matter how unfounded your child's fears may seem to you, they are very real to her, and no amount of telling her "There are no such things as monsters," or "Don't be silly. The toilet is not going to swallow you up," will dissuade her from her terror. And trying to force your child to overcome her fears—such as by insisting she pet the neighbor's dog or dunking her in the pool—will backfire, causing her to hold on to her fears for a longer time. She may even become clingy and frightened of other things if pushed to overcome a fear. A two-year-old simply does not have the ability to assimilate logic into her thinking.

Did you know?

Because young children spend nearly 80 percent of their sleep time in the "dream" sleep phase, they experience ten times as many nightmarish episodes a night as do adults, who spend only 8 to 10 percent of their sleep in this deep phase.

The best way to deal with your two-year-old's fears is to take a relaxed and respectful approach. By not making a big deal of the fears, they are likely to go away on their own in due time. If your child is terrified of swimming, for instance, refrain from trying to get her to understand that water won't hurt her. Instead, accept the fact that for whatever reason, water scares the daylights out of her, and wait until next year for swimming lessons. If it's clowns that make your child fearful, it's perfectly reasonable to find out ahead of time if there will be any clowns at her friends' birthday parties and to arrange for her to leave before the clown gets there or to arrive after the clown has left. And by all means, hold off on a trip to the circus.

If your child has nightmares, you may become so exhausted after being awakened several nights in a row by your fearful child that it may be tempting to allow her to crawl into bed with you, knowing that she'll fall back to sleep much more easily. But be wary of this arrangement. You want to avoid setting up a pattern where your child is unable to learn to comfort herself and go back to sleep on her own.

HELPING YOUR CHILD GROW
Overcoming fears

Most two-year-olds will outgrow their fears by the time they become preschoolers. If your child is afraid of something that cannot be avoided, such as thunder, bathwater, or a neighborhood dog you must pass every day, you might have to take a more active approach in helping her conquer her fear. To make sure your two-year-old's fears don't continue into later childhood—or even into adulthood—here are some things to try to help your child work through those things that frighten her:

Tell your child a story or read a book about the thing that frightens her. You can help desensitize your child to a fear by reading about a character who overcame his fears. Books showing topics in a benign setting, such as a lovable dog or a friendly spider, can help take some of the power away from the thing that scares her. Some books that deal with common childhood fears include:

♦ *The Monster Bed* by Jeanne Willis, illustrated by Susan Varley (Mulberry Books, 1999). Addresses fear of monsters and of the dark.

♦ *There's a Nightmare in My Closet* by Mercer Mayer (E. P. Dutton, 1992). Discusses fear of monsters, fear of the dark, and nightmares.

♦ *When the Big Dog Barks* by Munzee Curtis, illustrated by Susan Avashai (Greenwillow, 1997). About fear of strangers, dogs, and more.

♦ *I Don't Care, Said the Bear* by Colin West (Candlewick Press, 1997). About a fear of mice.

Give your child a feeling of control. The more active your child can be in controlling her fears, the sooner she will get them under control. For example, you can provide her with "Monster-Be-Gone," a plastic spray bottle filled with water or an air freshener that you've relabeled. Helping her spray it on window sills, under her bed and in her closet may help her feel as though she's taking action against the source of her fears. Other ideas include lining up stuffed animals and dolls as sentries to guard against an invasion, giving your child a flashlight to scare away the nighttime demons, helping her make a picture that clearly sends the message Monsters: Keep Out!, and conducting a monster search before bedtime. You might also ask your child what *she* thinks will keep the monsters away.

Limit your child's exposure to sources of potential fear. Since this age is ripe for developing fears, it's best to avoid exposing your child to those things you have control over that might generate fear, such as scary stories, scary movies and television shows, the nightly news, and violent cartoons.

Be a role model for your child. Tell your child that everyone has things they're afraid of—even grownups. Talk about what you were afraid of as a child and how you helped overcome your fears, being careful not to suggest new fears that your child may not have even thought of. Let her see you handle things calmly and with confidence even when they may frighten you.

Help build your child's confidence. Praise your child's efforts at overcoming her fears—no matter how small. If she feels brave enough to simply get her toes wet at the pool, for instance, then make sure you tell her how proud you are that she's feeling more comfortable around water. If, on the other hand, your child takes a backward step, be sure not to criticize her. And always make sure she knows that you love her and respect her, regardless of her fears.

Beware of introducing fears. Fear is contagious. If your child senses that you're anxious about something, she's likely to pick up on that fear and take it on as her own. Also, be wary of planting fears by saying things like "Don't be afraid of the water" if your child hasn't shown any fear.

For nightmares or bedtime fears
If bedtime and the dark are particular sources of your child's fears:

Encourage pretend play. If your child has recurring nightmares, you can help show her how she can calm the fears that may be lurking behind those bad dreams, in the safety and comfort of daylight. Pretend play allows your child to act out her emotions through her imagination. Your role is to encourage her play without being intrusive or directive or trying to act as a therapist or interpreter of your child's actions or feelings. Simply join your child, allow her to direct you, and be a good listener. Occasionally, you can ask her an open-ended question, such as "Why is the bear scared?" or "Why are your dolls fighting?" This will give your child an invitation to express more of what's on her mind. Be aware that your child probably will not act out her nightmare, as it may be too disturbing for her to talk about directly.

Maintain bedtime rituals. To help reduce nighttime anxiety and make your child feel more secure, create a set of pleasant routines you perform each night before putting your child to bed. Some children find it comforting to say goodnight to each of their stuffed animals and dolls. You might also try reading her a soothing story.

Gradually help your child to learn to comfort herself. If your child has been climbing into your bed late at night, looking for comfort after being awakened by a nightmare, think about putting a mattress or sleeping bag on the floor beside your bed. This will allow her to be close to you and provide her with a safe haven of her own. After a few nights of this, try coaxing her back to her own bed. Stay with her, gently soothing her, and holding her or rubbing her back until she falls back to sleep. The next time, sit beside your child, but use only your voice to comfort her. *Gradually* lessen your presence until your child is able to comfort herself back to sleep.

Making Halloween less scary

At Halloween, your two-year-old may be terrified when formerly familiar people put on masks and costumes and houses are transformed into scary places. At age two, she can't distinguish between make-believe and reality. To help your child deal with Halloween:

◆ Be sympathetic to her fears. Try to see the scary images through her eyes and realize how frightening they can seem.

◆ Don't expect your child to want to dress up, or to want to wear a costume you have picked out for her. She may, of course, want a costume, but if she doesn't, don't prod her.

◆ If your child is extremely fearful, don't take her trick-or-treating. Also avoid letting her come to the door with you to hand out treats.

◆ If you think your child will enjoy trick-or-treating, take her out before dark. Limit your outing to about a half hour and go only to the homes of neighbors, relatives, and friends. You may even want to limit the outing to one or two nearby homes. Avoid homes that are decorated in a particularly scary way.

◆ With other families, arrange a trick-or-treat party that's suited to two-year-olds. Children might go with parents to knock on different doors at home. Another parent can open the door and give out treats.

How I relate to people

How your two-year-old interacts with others

When your child was younger, he looked to his parents for everything. Mom and Dad could take care of all his needs: feeding him, changing him, comforting him, making him laugh. Now that he's becoming his own person, he needs to look beyond his nuclear family to learn how to act in the larger world. By broadening his circle of contacts to include siblings, playmates, extended family, caregivers, and even strangers, your child can begin to exercise his burgeoning independence, as well as try out newfound social skills. Through contact with others outside his immediate family, your child learns that there are numerous points of view and varying ways of doing things. He learns that each relationship fulfills different needs. Most of all, he'll feel more confident in the world if he sees himself as part of the larger community.

DEVELOPMENTAL MILESTONE
Developing friendships

Until recently, conventional wisdom said that two-year-olds were not capable of forming friendships, or even of interacting with each other, instead engaging in what experts termed "parallel play," which meant that they played side by side but did not interact with each other. It's now believed, however, that two-year-olds do interact in a more sophisticated fashion and indeed form friendships, however tenuous their relationships may be.

Around the time your child turns two, he will begin to notice that other children are just like him and he may even prefer the company of one child over another. If you take him to the playground, his eyes will light up and he will become more excited if he sees this particular playmate. When he's in a group of other children, he will tend to gravitate toward his friend. In a playgroup, he may sit near the door, waiting for his friend to arrive. If the friend fails to show up, your child may ask about her. When he plays with his friend, he may imitate what she does. If she's piling blocks on top of each other, your child will do the same, and most likely, in the same manner. This is a way for your child to tell his playmate, "I like you and I want to be like you."

What does your child learn from his playmates? To begin, it's a good feeling to be accepted by someone outside your immediate family. This helps your child gain confidence in himself. A friend also helps him begin to learn social skills, such as sharing, taking turns, and asking politely instead of grabbing. Of course, these skills have to be taught and do not come easily to two-year-olds. Also, because your child's buddy will most likely be close to his own age, he can play with someone whose skills and development are a close match to his own. This eliminates the frustration of not being able to keep up with an older sibling or not being able to do much with a baby sibling. And unlike brothers and sisters, friends are not vying for their parents' attention, so their disputes don't have the emotional baggage that siblings' fights do.

Other important relationships

Last year, your child focused all his emotional energy on his relationship with his parents. This year, in addition to relationships with peers, your child is ready to accept and be accepted by people in his extended family.

Grandparents. A relationship with his grandparents serves your child in many ways. With grandparents, your child experiences other adults who love him unconditionally, perhaps dote on him, and give him a sense of connection to an extended family. Most likely, your child leads a very structured life, with rules that he's expected to follow. Grandparents can provide a release from the structure of daily life. If you think of yourself as the guardian of your child's daily life, his grandparents are the accepting comforters. Because grandparents usually do not have to involve themselves in the day-to-day demands of child rearing, they can relate to your child in a way that is free of the stress of being a parent.

Grandparents can also influence your child's development in a self-affirming way. Children who are close to their grandparents feel accepted, even adored, and their lives are enriched immensely. Listening to a grandparent tell family stories and history, a child gains a sense of connection to the past and a feeling of security in the world outside the family. He begins to see himself as part of a greater whole. At the same time, however, two-year-olds can't quite figure out your relationship with your parents, since picturing you as a child is beyond their fertile imaginations. It's not that uncommon for an older two to ask, "Grandma, did you ever have any children?"

Siblings. Having a brother or sister is one of life's greatest joys—though it might not be readily apparent when your two-year-old and five-year-old are locked in a battle of wills. What does a sibling give your child? Brothers and sisters share so much more than the same parents and the same home. There's a shared history, shared jokes, shared experiences, and shared traditions. They watch and learn from each other: how to behave, how *not* to behave, the rewards for following the rules and the consequences of breaking them, what makes Mommy and Daddy happy and what makes them mad.

Siblings also teach each other a variety of skills. Often, an older child will help his younger brother or sister learn how to stack blocks, how to put a puzzle together, and how to negotiate for your time and attention. Your younger child gets important one-on-one time with someone older who will encourage him to test his skills and push himself further. The older sibling acts as a role model to the younger child who, in trying to keep up with his brother or sister, may take more risks and be more willing to venture away from his parents, gaining confidence and independence in the process.

A two-year-old with a younger sibling has the advantage of having someone around on a daily basis who can make him feel more confident, more capable, and more independent than he would without a baby sister or brother. Think of how proud he feels when he accomplishes something that his baby sibling has not yet learned to do! The baby is a barometer of sorts for how far he has come in just a couple of years. While a two-year-old still feels pretty vulnerable and somewhat helpless in the larger world, he feels extraordinarily powerful and capable compared to his younger sibling. Where his baby sister still babbles, he can actually talk in real sentences. The baby can't even get around by herself, yet he can walk and even run and climb. The baby can't feed herself, but he sure can navigate his way around a dinner plate. And when your two-year-old is given some age-appropriate responsibility for the baby—such as singing to her or fetching a diaper—he feels very important. The downside, in your two-year-old's mind, is great, however. The appearance of a baby just as he's beginning to become his own person may prompt him to believe that this is his punishment for "leaving you." Hence, his feelings about his new brother or sister may be quite mixed. He may be nurturing and caring one moment, and the next moment he may fly into a jealous rage because he believes you're giving the new baby too much attention at the expense of time with him.

When siblings are close in age, they learn from each other, which can be easier than learning from their parents. A five-year-old will use simpler language in talking to a two-year-old than will an adult. The frustration level with learning new skills from a sibling is lower, too, because their skills, as well as patience level, are more closely matched. Siblings often don't mind playing "mailman" over and over or going down the backyard slide a thousand times. Learning requires lots of energy and repetition, a natural part of children's play.

Caregivers. Forming a close bond with a caregiver encourages your child's growth in numerous ways. Being in the care of another adult for regular periods of time allows your child to develop his independence. Contrary to many parents' fears, young children know the difference between their parents and their caregivers and feel much greater intensity toward parents. If your child goes to his child-care provider for help solving a problem, it's a positive sign that he has developed a healthy trust in the world. It shows he's not afraid to venture past the immediate family to learn and find solutions. And it means he's becoming independent enough to know that he doesn't have to rely on his parents for virtually everything.

Your child's relationship with you

No other relationship is as central to your child's sense of well-being as is his relationship with his parents. Children gain an enormous amount from interacting on a daily basis with both their parents. To begin, each parent will naturally have their own distinct personality, taste, and style in how they relate to their child and approach their role as parent. Far from confusing your child, such differences expand his experiences and allow him to see that there are many ways to act and relate.

Also mothers and fathers tend to behave differently toward their children. Dads are more likely to relate to their children on a physical level—tossing them up in the air, getting on the floor and roughhousing, teaching them sports—while moms tend to talk to their children more and show their nurturing in more quiet ways. Fathers may challenge children to stretch their capabilities, while mothers offer a secure base of protection. Neither style is better or worse, but experiencing this variety enhances young children's experiences.

CONFLICT
Social graces versus emotional needs

Ask a two-year-old to share his new teddy bear with his playmate, and you're likely to see his grip on the toy tighten, the look in his face harden, and hear a piercing, "No! Mine!" It's not that your child is selfish or inconsiderate. To children this age, the concept of sharing is completely alien. As they see it, possession really *is* nine-tenths of the law, and if something's in their hands, they will cling to it ferociously. In fact, your child's definition of sharing goes something like "What's mine is mine and what's yours is mine."

It doesn't matter if yanking his playmate's favorite truck away will lead to an all-out war; your two-year-old sees this as simply the price to pay for claiming his own property. He doesn't see this as greed or bad behavior, either. On the contrary, two-year-olds believe that *all* objects—even those belonging to others—are an extension of themselves. And because two-year-olds are just beginning to develop a sense of identity, to surrender an item to anyone else is to relinquish a part of themselves.

How it feels to be me

Because children are very concrete and their sense of time is still largely undeveloped, they have tremendous difficulty understanding that if they let a playmate have their toy for a while, they will get it back later. Here's what might be going through your child's mind when you ask him to share:

What do you mean I should share my brand new pail and shovel with Justin? No way! If I let Justin have it, it's not mine anymore. I love my pail and shovel. How could you ask me to give it away—especially when you bought it for me? It doesn't make any sense that you would buy me a special gift and then tell me I have to give it away. You say I can have it back later, but you might as well say never.

I'm going to hold on to this pail and shovel as tight as I can and not let Justin—or anyone else—take it from me, because I want it to stay mine. Let Justin get his own pail and shovel!

YOU AND YOUR CHILD
Sharing your child

Now that your child is broadening his interactions, it may be hard on you to share your role as the center of his life. After all, up until now, your child depended on you for everything. You could meet all his physical, as well as emotional, needs. But as his world expands, some of those needs can be met through others: a grandparent may comfort him, a sibling may teach him new skills, a playmate may entertain him, a caregiver may feed and clothe him and show him affection. A decrease in this all-encompassing role in your child's life may give you a sense of loss. Yet you may also feel a degree of relief that some of the pressure of being all things to your child has been lifted.

The caregiver-child relationship is probably the most difficult one for parents to reconcile. On the one hand, you want your child to have a close, nurturing relationship with the person entrusted to look after him in your absence. On the other hand, you may be afraid that if he gets *too* close, he may view his caregiver as more important in his life than you are. You may even start to wonder whether your child knows the difference between his parent and his baby-sitter—especially if your child slips and calls his caregiver "Mommy." Relax! Such fears are usually unfounded, although every parent probably experiences them at some point. Your child knows the difference, even if he's unable to articulate it through words. Your child also knows that you will always be there for him. If you find yourself worried or jealous that your child goes to his caregiver to help solve a problem or fix a scraped knee, rest assured that he's not rejecting your wisdom or starring role in his life. On the contrary, it shows that he's gaining independence from his family and becoming his own person. And if he shows deep affection for his baby-sitter, take it as a good sign that you made the right choice.

Your child's close relationship with his grandparents may also trigger ambivalent feelings in you—especially if their approach to child rearing differs from yours. You may worry that your parents or in-laws are spoiling your child or confusing him with rules that differ from your own. But children can easily negotiate the differences.

If you've had a difficult relationship with your parents, you may even feel resentful that they are giving your child the kind of unconditional love and support that you felt was lacking when you were growing up. Or they may simply indulge your child, as opposed to being the strict parents they were to you. Rather than feeling bitter, instead try to see that your parents may be looking to your child to provide *them* with a second chance to be loving, giving parents. Your parents may even have come to realize that they had shortcomings and want to work hard to correct these shortcomings with their grandchildren. However your child's grandparents choose to express their love for him, step back and, as long as they are not putting him in any danger, allow them to develop a full and meaningful relationship with your child. Your child can only benefit from a close bond with his grandparents.

When your child sees you and your spouse behave lovingly toward each other, he learns to expand his own sense of safety with both parents, even as he may feel jealousy. When he sees conflict, he feels less secure. While you don't want to give your child the impression that conflict between spouses is something that must be avoided at all costs, you do want to show him that you can resolve your differences with love and respect. (One area about which you should avoid showing any conflict in front of your child, however, is discipline. You don't want to confuse your child or create a situation where he can play one parent off another.)

Mothers sometimes have a difficult time with their child's relationship with the father. It's not that they don't *want* their child to have a close relationship, but it can feel threatening to allow the father to parent in his own way. In fact, a mother may unconsciously prevent the father from parenting by questioning what he is doing, involving herself in the process, and not allowing him to take charge and share the responsibility for their child. On the contrary, if a mother steps back and allows a father to parent in his own way, the child feels that both parents are there for him. Encouraging parents who nurture their children, with the space to do it in their own ways, creates a good role model for both boys and girls.

Whatever your feelings, it's important that you help your child's circle grow and encourage him to bond with other family members and learn to trust those outside the family.

HELPING YOUR CHILD GROW
Enhancing his relationships

This year, as your child's social circle extends beyond you, you can help him form relationships with his peers and extended family.

Teaching your child to share

Teaching the concept of sharing to a two-year-old is not easy. Sharing takes practice, persistence, and patience, but it's the foundation of your child's developing friendships. Here's how you can help:

Teach your child the concept of ownership. Look for natural opportunities to let your child know that some things belong to him and some things belong to others. "This is your tricycle. This book is Mommy's. Look at Daddy's watch. That's Ashley's doll."

Show him that when he gives something away, he'll get it back. Using an object that has no value or meaning to your child, such as a paper cup, show your child how reciprocity works. "I give you the cup. Now you give Mommy the cup. Now Mommy gives the cup to you." Or, sit on the floor opposite your child and gently roll a ball to him, saying, "I'm giving you the ball." As he rolls it back, say, "Now you roll the ball back to me." You can work up to objects that have more meaning to him, each time holding on to the item for a little longer, but keeping it within his sight. This will show him that if he gives something up, it will not be taken away forever.

You can use these games as examples when you encourage your child to share his toys with a playmate: "Remember when you gave Mommy your bunny and you got it back? If you let Janine play with your truck, you'll get that back, too."

Acknowledge your child's feelings. Suppose your child has gotten into a tug-of-war over a shovel in the sandbox. Rather than trying to force your child to relinquish the object, let him know that you understand him. Say, "I see you really want that shovel. I know it's sometimes hard to share. When you're finished, maybe you can let your friend play with it for a while. Are you done using it now or would you like to use it a little longer?" By articulating your child's feelings, you let him know that you understand him, which may help him overcome his reluctance to share. You are also encouraging him to share in a way that doesn't make him feel bad. You are allowing *him* to make the decision rather than have it be forced on him. To be sure, he may not immediately hand over the coveted object to his playmate, but he will eventually get the message that sharing can enhance rather than diminish his play experiences.

Don't force your child to share everything. Children need to know that some things are theirs and theirs alone. After all, don't you have certain possessions you would never lend out? A piece of jewelry with sentimental attachment? A new car? An author-signed edition of a special book? If your child knows there are some things that are off-limits to others, he'll be more apt to share his less important possessions. Be careful not to put him in a position where he'll have to defend his special item from another child's inquisitive hands. If he doesn't want to share his brand-new fire truck, for instance, make sure it's out of reach when other children come over to play.

You and your child's in-home caregiver

If your child is in the care of an in-home caregiver during the day, you'll have to work hard to make sure that the relationship between you and the caregiver is professional and mutually respectful. Unlike a child-care center or nursery school where the relationship is more formally spelled out, you and your child's caregiver will have to negotiate your own terms. The more positive your relationship is with the caregiver, the better it will be for your child and for you. If you consider the caregiver a partner with you and operate from a basis of mutual trust and respect, she will give your child the attention, care, and love that you would want him to receive in your absence. To help establish a comfortable, productive relationship:

• **Clearly outline the parameters of the job.** Before your caregiver begins, sit down with her and tell her everything you expect of her, including if you want her to do any housework in addition to looking after your child. Discuss the hours, what and when she will be paid, benefits, vacations, and additional compensation for overtime. Then put it all in writing.

• **Agree on rules and methods of discipline.** It's important that your caregiver acts in a way that's consistent with your parenting philosophy, but avoid getting nitpicky about the small stuff. Dressing your child in mismatched hat and mittens when you're a stickler for color

Don't expect your child to share when a new baby arrives. Often, children get very possessive of their own belongings upon the arrival of a new sibling as a reaction to being forced to share their parents. This is especially true if your two-year-old is a first-born. Instead of making your child feel selfish for not wanting to share his things, let him know that you understand how he feels and give him plenty of reassurance: "I know Mommy and Daddy are giving the baby a lot of attention right now. But we still love you just as much as ever." Then be sure to give your two-year-old some one-on-one time.

coordination, or slipping him a piece of candy every now and then when you have strict rules about sweets, is not going to undermine your parenting and won't have any real effect on your child—unless you turn it into an issue.

• **Show consideration for your caregiver's time.** If she expects to end her day by 6:00 P.M., then make every effort to arrive home at that time. If you anticipate being late, call her. And make sure you compensate her for any time she's worked over her regular hours. If you'd like her to watch your child on a day that she normally has off, give her enough notice so she can make arrangements. And don't be upset if she can't make it. Remember, your child's caregiver has a life—and perhaps a family—of her own.

• **Treat her with the same respect you'd expect yourself.** Speak to the caregiver the same way you'd speak to any adult you consider your equal. Avoid correcting her in front of your child; you don't want to undermine her authority. If you need to discuss an issue, do it in private and be willing to give her opportunities to air any concerns she has.

It's also important that you respect your caregiver's beliefs and cultural practices if they're different from yours, unless they interfere with your child's well-being. Keep in mind that exposure to different ideas and cultures benefits your child.

Teach your child how to take turns. Taking turns is a way of sharing things that don't belong to your child, such as the slide at the playground or a place in line. To help your child learn that others have rights, too, insist that he wait his turn to go on the slide and that he not shove himself in front of other children at the ice-cream truck. As your child learns these social graces it becomes easier for him to share both space and actual objects with others.

Let your child see you share. When you set an example of sharing and generosity, your child will follow your lead. Be sure to let him know what you're doing. For instance, "These are my hedge clippers, but we're letting Mr. McWilliams borrow them." Or, "These cookies of mine are yummy. Would you like me to share some with you?"

Reduce possibilities of conflict over sharing. If you're hosting a playdate, keep strife to a minimum by making sure you have enough toys to go around. You might ask the other parents to bring along toys and have multiples of certain favorites on hand. Don't provide playthings that can be used by only one child at a time and may promote conflict, such as a single riding toy. Instead, have large play structures that several children can use at once. Even something as simple as a couple of large cartons, pillows, and a blanket will do. The children can take turns jumping in, hiding, and coming up with all sorts of fun games. Art supplies, too, encourage more peaceful play than one-of-a-kind dolls and toys.

Praise your child when he shares. Your child wants your approval. When you say, "That was very nice of you to let your friend play with your ball," he'll take note of that and be more apt to repeat his sharing in the future. But don't expect too much. It takes a long time for children to get into the habit of generosity.

Helping your two-year-old bond with a new sibling

Expect that your child will feel some sense of displacement when a younger sibling arrives. To ease the transition and help him see the newcomer as an interesting addition to his life rather than the source of all his new troubles:

Refer to his new sibling as "our" baby. Besides helping your two-year-old feel more included, this will avoid causing him to feel as though the baby is replacing him. Seeing his new brother or sister as "his baby" will help make him feel like a "proud parent" rather than a displaced older child. He'll also feel more included if you let him introduce the new baby to visitors.

Allow your child to hold the baby. Having close physical contact will help your child develop a loving bond with his new brother or sister. If you're worried that your two-year-old will drop the baby, you can have him sit on the floor while cradling the baby in his lap. Make sure you are close by at all times to ensure your infant's safety.

Let your child help you take care of the baby. Even a two-year-old can be of some assistance when you're changing the baby's diaper or feeding her. Ask your child to hand you items as you change the baby's diaper or occasionally spread a blanket on the floor and encourage your two-year-old to gently amuse the baby while you change her diaper. Ask him to sing to the baby as you feed her. As your two-year-old watches you care for the new baby, let him know that you did the same things for him when he was a newborn. Point out how much he has grown since then.

Be sure to give your two-year-old special attention. It's easy to get caught up in the daily drama of taking care of a newborn. To make sure your two-year-old doesn't feel brushed aside and resentful of his new sibling, enlist friends and family members to watch the baby while you spend some one-on-one time with your older child. Try to spend this time away from the baby, if possible, so you can give your two-year-old your undivided attention. You can go to the park or just to another room of the house. Let him know that he is just as important to you as he was before the baby was born.

Catch your child being a good sibling. Whenever your two-year-old willingly shares with his sibling or shows empathy or caring, make sure you let him know how proud you are of him by saying, for instance, "I saw how gentle you were with the new baby. She's very lucky to have such a good brother." The more you acknowledge his positive interactions with his sibling, the more likely he is to repeat them.

Don't ask him to share with the baby. Now is not the time to review lessons on sharing as far as the new arrival is concerned. Don't displace your two-year-old from his crib to make room for the baby. If he's ready to move on to a toddler bed, make the switch before the baby arrives or months later, after the baby's presence is not such a novelty. Don't insist that he pass along a toy, even a rattle that he's long ago lost interest in, to the baby. If you're using your two-year-old's outgrown clothing for your infant, there's no need to share that information.

Building the connection with grandparents

If your parents or in-laws live far away, or you have your own difficulties with them, you don't want these obstacles to interfere with your child's relationship with his grandparents. Here are some approaches to help your child form a close connection.

Encourage grandparents to spend time alone with your child. Let your child get to know his grandparents on his own terms, without you acting as a go-between. This allows your child to develop special rituals and experiences that are different from what he's used to at home.

Don't let your child hear you criticize his grandparents. If you feel they are violating your rules, wait to discuss your concerns with your parents or in-laws when they're out of earshot of your child. And don't discuss any negative feelings you may have about them in front of your child. You don't want your experiences to influence how your child feels about his grandparents.

Make an effort to keep in touch. When grandparents live too far away for frequent visits, it can be a challenge to foster a strong grandparent-grandchild bond. Seeing their grandparents only once or twice a year for the holidays is not enough for young children to develop a strong relationship with them. Children need something to remind them of their grandparents even when they're not around.

While regular phone calls can help, you need to go further to keep your child connected since phone calls are more of a game with two-year olds than a means of communication. You might ask grandparents to tape record or videotape themselves reading a favorite book to your child. While they're at it, have them record family stories or even songs or lullabies. Get out your camcorder and tape your child showing off his latest achievement. Have your child make cards or drawings to send to his grandparents or dictate a letter to them. Make a family tree with pictures of all the members and hang it where your child can see it. If you and your child's grandparents have access to the Internet, build a home page and scan in pictures to send back and forth.

Let your child know continually that he is connected to a larger family. Look for opportunities to include mentions of grandparents in your conversations with your child. "I'm making the soup that Grandma used to make for me when I was a little girl"; "Your Grandpa loves birds, too"; "You have the same smile as Grandma."

You want your child to be open to new people and experiences. Some children, however, have a tendency to rush off in search of new acquaintances or be too quick to trust strangers. A two-year-old can't yet make the distinction between good and bad strangers and may put himself in jeopardy. While you don't want to frighten him, you can teach him some personal safety.

If your child...	Do say	Don't say
runs away from you	"Our rule is no running away in a department store."	"Don't ever run away from me again. Something terrible could happen."
is offered a piece of candy by a stranger on the bus	"Always ask Mommy first if it's okay."	"Never take anything from a stranger."
shows off her new doll to an admiring woman in the checkout line	"That's nice of you to show your dolly to the nice lady."	"Don't talk to strangers."

Teaching your child about bad strangers at this age is a little premature because a two-year-old should never be out of adult supervision. Rather than giving your child the message that people are bad, you need to teach your child, "You must always stay where I can see you."

My body, my self

Your two-year-old's body and gender awareness

When your child was an infant and first discovered her hands, she would hold them in front of her face, slowly moving her arms as though she were doing tai chi. She was fascinated by these mysterious objects. And her feet! Well, when she discovered those, it was like getting a new toy to put in her mouth. This may not have been the most practical use for her appendages, but it certainly helped her become more familiar with her body parts.

Now that your child is two, she continues to explore her body, but in a more purposeful way. She's figuring out how her body is made and in the process, identifying which actions are pleasurable. And now that she's beginning to use the toilet and her body is often freed from the confines of a diaper, she discovers her genitals. Here's a part of her body that heretofore went barely noticed. This new discovery is a source of pride and wonder—and your child will most likely want to share it with anyone else who might be interested. Don't be surprised if she rips off her diaper (usually in the company of guests) and announces, "Ta da!" as though she has just performed a magic trick. And like a performer, she expects to be admired and applauded for her efforts.

It's not uncommon for two-year-olds to spend much of their waking hours with their hands down their pants. Sexual curiosity isn't necessarily what prompts their explorations. Rather, it is more of a scientific exploration of this newly discovered body part. Your child wants to find out everything she can about it, just as she once spent time exploring her fingers and toes. Of course, children also find out that touching their penis or vagina feels good, so naturally, they want to do it again—and again. Besides the obvious pleasure it brings, masturbation can also act as a self-soothing mechanism, just as sucking on a pacifier or thumb did when they were infants. This is a natural part of the growing process.

DEVELOPMENTAL MILESTONE
Noticing gender differences

Sometime between the ages of two and three, children begin to notice distinctions between the sexes. This is a natural outgrowth of your child's emerging sense of identity. Once she begins to be aware of her own physical characteristics, she naturally becomes keenly interested in those of others and how they differ from hers. Anatomical differences are usually the first attributes that two-year-olds notice, and investigating and comparing each other's genitals and the idea of gender becomes a big adventure.

It's around this time that children also begin to act in gender-specific ways. Despite parents' best efforts to encourage "gender-neutral" roles and games, girls and boys will show a decided preference for certain play and behaviors. Girls often will play with dolls, act in nurturing ways, dress up as princesses, and play house. Boys will gravitate toward toy trucks and play tools, dress as superheroes, and act in generally more physically aggressive ways. Their play may show signs of sexism that would make many a modern-day parent cringe: the role of Mommy calls for domestic play; the role of Daddy calls for engagement in matters mechanical. Where does all this gendered role-playing come from? From watching their parents and other adults, of course. No matter how enlightened parents believe they are about male-female behavior, most people still act in gender-specific ways, and children are keen observers and imitators of their parents and other adults in their circle. Even at this early age, the media, too, influences your child's understanding of what it is to be a boy or a girl.

The body as factory
The body can produce an amazing variety of "products" in every molecular configuration, and this discovery is a source of fascination and pride for your two-year-old. First, there's the solid matter, such as feces. Then there's the liquid matter of urine and tears, and the in-between stuff of mucus and spit. Finally, there's the gases: burps and farts—particularly fascinating because of the sounds that accompany them! In an attempt to learn more about these bodily products, your child may act in bizarre ways: letting urine run over her hand, piling up a mound of spit on her plate, smearing feces on the bathroom wall, picking her nose and tasting the mucus, and announcing for all the world to hear: "I farted!"

To the relief of most parents, these experiments are usually short-lived. In the meantime, it helps to keep in mind that your child's fascination with and experiments on the stuff that comes out of her body is no different to her than examining the texture of oatmeal or seeing what she can do with a ball of modeling clay. Her body is just one more territory to conquer in her quest for knowledge about the world around her.

How it feels to be me

Children frequently have their first haircut around the age of two. Of course, this is the time that coincides with your child's fierce attachment to her hair, as well as her nails, and her desire to control her fate. Here's what might be going through your child's mind as you prop her up on the haircutter's chair:

Why are you trying to change me? This is my hair and now you're taking it away from me. Why does it have to be cut, anyway? I like it just the way it is. But now you take me to this strange place with yucky smells and put me in a big, stiff chair, and this stranger makes my hair all wet. It's cold and I don't like the way it feels when this stranger combs it. And then there's the scissors! You're always telling me to stay away from scissors and sharp objects, and now this person is coming right at me with these really pointy ones. What if he pokes my eye out?

As I watch the floor pile up with my hair, I get really mad. That was mine! Now I don't even look like the same me. I want my hair back!

CONFLICT
Choosing a gender identity

Your two-year-old's emerging gender awareness does not mean that she fully accepts and understands the differences. Many two-year-olds believe that they are both genders at once. Girls are often convinced they have a penis, while boys want breasts to suckle a baby. In fact, boys may be under the mistaken belief that they'll grow breasts and even become pregnant when they become adults, just like their mommy. Likewise, girls may believe that they'll grow a penis when they get older. If your daughter has seen her brother or a male playmate urinate while standing, she may try to do the same. Your child's understanding of gender may also be inconsistent. Ask her if she's a girl or a boy and her answer is likely to change from day to day. As in other areas of their lives, two-year-olds simply refuse to accept the constraints imposed on them. As they see it, even biology is something they can overcome!

Your child's emerging gender awareness can also be cause for anxiety. A boy, upon witnessing a girl's diaper being changed, may grow fearful that he could lose his penis. Remember, he knows that things that come out of the body (feces) get whisked away with the diaper change, so it's not such a stretch for him to conclude that things *attached* to the body (his penis) might also disappear. Girls might also become anxious over not having the same equipment as boys. It's not necessarily that they want what boys have (according to Freud's classic theory of "penis envy"), but more that they wonder what happened to their "own" penis.

Two-year-olds' body anxieties extend beyond gender to include bodily functions. In some cases, bowel movements and urination can make a child feel uncomfortable because her body is doing something she cannot control. And if your child is prone to digestive cramps, diarrhea, or constipation, she might feel as though her body was attacking her from the inside. Toilet-teaching, if it is imposed on her before she is ready to learn, can be a source of anxiety because she feels as though she has no authority over her body. Therefore, she may feel shame for having disappointed her parents.

Also, because your child sees her body as sacred, she may become upset if you try to alter any part, such as cutting her hair or trimming her nails. No amount of explaining that her hair and nails will grow back will appease her. In her view, you're taking away part of her body, as well as taking away her control over it.

Issues surrounding food can also be understood by your child as an assault on the primacy of her body. If, for instance, you insist that she eat something she doesn't want, she may feel that her body is being invaded. It's best to let your child choose how much of anything she wants to eat, making the point that food is used to build a strong body and should be eaten to satisfy hunger, not to satisfy you.

Gender confusion and gender roles

It may be disconcerting to you when your son declares that he's going to have a baby and breast-feed him "just like mommy" or your daughter insists that she will grow a penis when she grows up. And when your child "crosses" gender in more extreme ways, such as if your daughter runs around dangling a carrot in front of her vagina or your son holds a baby doll to his chest as he imitates breast-feeding, you may feel downright upset. But remember that just as it takes a long time for your child to understand the concepts of numbers and time, so it takes a while for her to understand the concept of gender. There's bound to be confusion until your child understands that gender is something fixed and that one is either a girl or a boy and each has different attributes that stay that way throughout their lives.

Haircuts without tears

To help your child's haircuts be less traumatic, follow these tips:

Look for a barbershop or hair salon that caters to kids. You want a haircutter who's patient with children and who understands their reluctance to alter their appearance.

Visit the hair salon or barber before your child's appointment. If possible, let your child watch you get your hair cut or other children get theirs cut so she'll be able to see that people survive haircuts. It will also make the place more familiar to her, and you can answer any questions she may have. One note of caution: Don't stick around if another child is screaming his head off while the barber works. This model will not comfort your child.

Let your child see that hair grows. Show her pictures from when she was younger, as well as pictures of any siblings or yourself that show hair at different lengths.

Schedule something fun for after the haircut. Your child may be more willing to cooperate if she knows you've planned a trip to a children's museum, a park, or a visit with a friend following the haircut. Don't set up the outing as a reward for her cooperation, but simply as one of the interesting things on her agenda today. This way, you'll get her attention off the haircut and on something she enjoys. Remind her of the planned activity during the haircut.

Invite your child to watch as you or your spouse gets a haircut. This serves two purposes: (1) she gets to see what the process is like and that you enjoy it, and (2) she isn't later startled to find you with a changed appearance, a situation that could frighten her.

YOU AND YOUR CHILD
Handling your feelings about masturbation

It can be very disconcerting for you to watch your child fondle her genitals. Yet, when she was an infant and spent hours exploring her fingers and toes, you delighted in her discoveries as much as she did. But children's fascination with their genitals—as well as the genitals of their playmates—makes many parents uncomfortable.

It's important to understand that all your child's explorations are natural, and a normal part of development. And though she does derive pleasure from her actions—that's why she keeps going back—the pleasure is not sexual in nature. Fondling her genitals is as innocent to her as putting her finger in her belly button, playing with her toes, or pulling on her earlobe. That's why you should never make your child feel ashamed for her actions. Scolding her or trying to get her to stop will confuse her and she will get the idea that it's bad or forbidden to have those good feelings, instead of normal and healthy.

How you respond to your child's behavior will shape both her sexual values and self-esteem. While you would not purposefully try to make your child feel ashamed, you could unconsciously transmit the idea that her sex play disgusts or embarrasses you. She then may get the idea not only that her body is something to be ashamed of, but that she, as a person, is bad. That's why it's imperative that the way you act reassures your child and makes her feel a sense of respect for herself, as well as for others.

As accepting as you may be about your child's genital play, you may feel like disappearing into the woodwork if your child begins fondling herself in public. Be careful, however, about scolding her or making her feel embarrassed. You want her to understand that there's nothing wrong with her behavior, but there are some things, like touching her genitals, that are okay to do in private but are not okay to do in public. This concept may take her a while to grasp, and you may find her slipping her hand into her pants on a future outing. Without embarrassing her, gently remind her what you talked about. Finding a distraction to occupy her hands can also be helpful.

It's not uncommon for parents suddenly to feel self-conscious about their own sexuality when their child begins to become more aware of her own genitals and ask questions. Even if you've previously been fairly relaxed about nudity, you may now find yourself reaching for a bathrobe after your shower, or closing the door to the bathroom when you're on the toilet. That doesn't mean that you've suddenly become prudish. In fact, it's a good idea now to keep your genitals from your child's view. Not only are adult genitals at eye level to a two-year-old, they are much larger than your child's, which could make her feel overwhelmed.

HELPING YOUR CHILD GROW
Laying the groundwork for sexual health

You are your child's first and foremost sex educator. Age two is not too early to begin to lay the foundation for helping your child to grow into a sexually healthy adult.

Masturbation

Masturbation in itself is a normal part of growing up and not a behavior problem. Some genital play is perfectly normal. However, some children use self-stimulation not as a source of pleasure and exploration, but to soothe themselves from underlying anxiety.

If your child seems to spend an excessive amount of time fondling her genitals or engaging in sex play with others, something could be making her anxious. Look to see if there have been any recent changes that might be causing your child some distress, such as a move, entering nursery school, a new baby-sitter, or the birth of a sibling. Ask yourself if there has been any tension at home that your child might be picking up on. Once these factors are dealt with, and your child is reassured, you should see a lessening of the frequency of her masturbation.

However, if your child seems obsessed with her genitals, seems fearful or distressed, and you can't determine the source of her stress, you need to address this problem with a professional.

Teach your child the names of sexual organs. Just as you help your child learn the names of her other body parts, you should give her the correct name for her genitals. This is a good opportunity to emphasize that when she's in public, she should refrain from naming her sexual organs, instead referring to them as her "private parts" if she needs to talk about them.

Respect your child's boundaries. There may be times when your child doesn't want to cuddle or kiss. Respect her wishes and don't force her or make her feel bad. When you show your child you respect her boundaries, she learns to respect her own boundaries and learns that it's okay to say "No" to people. This will protect her as she gets older because she will learn to pay attention to her own desires, rather than giving in to someone else's demands.

Avoid tickling. Tickling is overstimulating and frightening to a child. The automatic reaction of laughter is not an emotional response that says, "I'm enjoying this." It's a purely physical response and it confuses your child to laugh when in fact she is not having fun. Gentle playful tickles that your child can easily escape from, of course, are harmless.

Teach by example. There's no better way to teach your child about loving, respectful relationships than to show her how by the way you and your spouse interact. Don't be afraid to be affectionate in front of your child. When your child witnesses her parents hugging, kissing, and acting thoughtfully and lovingly toward each other, she sees real love in action. Any jealousy she feels is part of her need to share in that love.

Answering your child's questions

There's an old joke about a little boy who asked, "Mommy, where did I come from?" The mother, wanting to give her son a truthful answer, launched into a scientific discussion of eggs and sperm and the process of birth. After a pause, her confused son shrugged his shoulders and said, "Oh. Timmy said he came from Cleveland, and I was just wondering where I came from."

Parents sometimes answer their children's questions with far more detail than they need or want to know. Two-year-olds are simply too young to digest all that information and may actually end up being discomfited or confused by too much detail. At this age it's best to keep your answers short and simple. When your child wants more information, she'll ask. Let your child know you're glad she asked, and answer her in a calm, matter-of-fact way. Following are some of the most common questions two-year-olds ask, and some suggested responses:

Where do babies come from? "Before a baby is born, she grows inside her mommy in a special place in her mommy's body."

How does the baby get out? "When the baby has grown big enough, she moves out of her mommy's body." If your child understands what a vagina is, then you can say that the baby "comes out through the mommy's vagina."

What's that? Can I touch it? "That's Mommy's vagina [or Daddy's penis]. That's a special place that's private. I don't want you to touch it. Mommy and Daddy touch you when we change your diaper or give you a bath, and the doctor touches it when he checks you. But that's a person's own special place and nobody else should touch it."

Why don't I have a penis? "Girls don't have penises. They have vaginas. That's one of the differences between girls and boys."

Why can't boys have babies? "Only girls can get pregnant and have babies. But boys help make the babies. And they help take care of them after they're born."

Why isn't my penis as big as Daddy's? (or Why don't I have breasts like Mommy?) "Because Daddy is all grown up, he's much taller than you. His hands and feet are also bigger than yours. When you grow up, you'll be tall like Daddy and everything else will be bigger—including your penis."

Don't be surprised if your child asks the same questions repeatedly. These are complicated concepts for two-year-olds to understand. Like all other concepts though, eventually your child will catch on.

Broadening your child's view of gender

To become emotionally healthy adults, children need to develop a strong sense of what it means to be a male or female without limiting themselves to stereotypical notions of masculinity or femininity. As a parent, you want to cultivate your child's understanding of her gender without limiting her potential. Here's how you can help your child explore the full range of her personality:

Set an example. Do you and your spouse act according to traditional roles for the sexes? If so, your child will get a clear message about gender roles: women cook, do housework, and take care of the children; men go to work and take care of the yard. But, if your child sees you dividing your chores less rigidly, and doing a wide range of things, she will be less likely to adopt a narrow view of gender.

Encourage nonstereotypical behavior. Support your son's nurturing instincts. If you have an infant, let him tend his new sibling. Praise him when he shows empathy to another child. Let him know that it's okay to cry. By the same token, cheer your daughter when she performs physical feats. Allow her to enjoy roughhousing. Support her interest in things mechanical or scientific.

Don't limit your child to gender-specific toys. Sure, boys love trucks and girls love dolls. And there's no reason they shouldn't play with these toys. But if your daughter shows an interest in a gleaming new fire truck, or your son asks for the latest baby doll, encourage them to play with these things. Don't try to force certain toys on your child in an effort to broaden her notion of gender, though. It's also a good idea to look for toys that are gender neutral. Learning toys such as puzzles and blocks are a great example, as are toys that are centered on a theme, such as a farm play set or school play set.

Read books that show men and women or boys and girls acting in nontraditional ways. There are many wonderful books—especially older books—that show men and women acting only in traditional ways. To balance those images, read your child books that show mothers going to work and fathers nurturing children, women working with tools and men doing housework, and females who are athletes and males who pursue the arts.

It's important that you teach your child proper boundaries about public displays of her body without making her feel ashamed. Here are some situations common to two-year-olds, and the best way to respond to them:

If your child...	Do say	Don't say
is touching a playmate's genitals	Nothing at first, but calmly redirect the children into another activity. Later, tell your child, "It's not a good idea to touch anyone else's private parts or let anyone else touch yours."	"Stop that! That's not nice."
puts her hands down her pants in public	"I know it feels good when you touch yourself. It's okay to do that when you're alone, but not okay to do it in front of others. It's private."	"Bad girl. Don't ever do that again."

It's potty time!

Your two-year-old and toilet-learning

Remember when your child made the leap from crawling to walking and from babbling to using real words? Those were huge developmental milestones, worthy of hauling out the camcorder and making a record of your child's achievements. Another leap in development comes when your formerly diaper-dependent child learns to use the potty. And while the transition from diapers to the toilet may be more uneven and less dramatic than those first steps and first words, and perhaps is not something you want to record on video for posterity, it is a major step in growing up.

Your toddler's readiness for toilet-learning

By the time your child turns two, he may be ready to learn to use the potty. The average for toilet-learning is two years and eight months, although some children are not ready until after they turn three, and some show signs of readiness before their second birthday. Age, then, is *not* the criteria for toilet readiness. A child will learn to use the potty only when he develops the inner control and interest he'll need to teach herself.

Your child has many ways of signaling to you that he's ready to begin learning to use the potty. He is most likely ready to begin toilet-learning if he shows several of the following signs:

The ability to use and understand language. Your child should be able to follow simple directions, such as "Sit down on the potty seat." He should also be able to name the different parts of his body, as well as understand words that apply to using the potty, such as "wet," "clean," "dry," "potty," and whatever words you choose to label the urination and defecation processes. Additionally, he should have a clear understanding of what the potty is used for.

Curiosity about the toileting process. Your child may start to follow you or his siblings into the bathroom and ask questions about bathroom habits. He may also want to see what's in his wet or dirty diapers.

Discomfort with diapers. Your child may tug at his diapers after soiling them. He may even ask to be changed.

Physical control. Indications that your child has the neuromuscular control necessary for learning to use the potty include waking up dry in the morning or after naps, staying dry for long periods during the day, having fairly regular bowel movements (usually 15 to 20 minutes after a meal), pausing just before having a bowel movement, and being able to pull elasticized pants up and down.

An interest in doing things himself. Your child may show all the signs of readiness mentioned above, but unless he has a desire to master tasks alone, you'll find yourself frustrated in trying to teach him to use the potty.

CONFLICT
Which urge to give in to?

When you begin teaching your child to use the potty, he knows what is expected of him and looks forward to the time when he can stay clean and dry. But he must mount a number of obstacles to get to that point, and accidents are a normal part of the process. Feeling stressed, tired, excited, or distracted can all cause toileting lapses, even when he's made substantial progress. Adjusting to a new sibling or the start of preschool or any other changes in his routine can also affect his consistency in toileting.

Your child's physical control may also not be caught up to his understanding of using the potty. It's not uncommon for a child to sit on the potty with no results, only to wet himself right afterward. Your child isn't being defiant. On the contrary, he's associating the potty with elimination. It's just that he does not yet have the ability to time his bodily functions to the act of sitting on the potty.

Your child may also be fairly good at urinating in the potty, but withhold his bowel movements. This is most likely due to certain fears he has because he does not yet understand how the body works. He may fear the sensation of letting go of his BMs because it feels as though he's losing a part of himself. He may even worry that the rest of him may follow suit.

Another conflict for your child is choosing which urge to follow when the sensation of needing the potty hits him. If he's engaged in a fun activity, he has to make a choice: Should he stop what he's doing and use the potty or just continue with his fun? Sometimes he'll choose the potty. Sometimes not.

How it feels to be me

Children often have a difficult time understanding why they have to learn to use the potty. Here's what might be going through your child's mind as he tries to get the hang of using a potty seat:

Why are they making me do this on a chair? I've been making in my diaper ever since I can remember and up till now, everyone has seemed pleased. So what's changed? I don't get why this way is supposed to be better. The other way, I didn't have to stop whatever I was doing so I could make. Now I have to sit on this chair at certain times of the day and wait for something to happen. And more times than not, nothing happens! And then sometimes I end up making a mess all over myself and the floor. That never happened before I had to sit on this chair. Wouldn't everything just be easier if I could continue to use my diaper?

On the other hand, those diapers can be pretty uncomfortable when I've wet or pooped in them. Maybe I should give this a try.

YOU AND YOUR CHILD
Toilet-teaching without tears

It cannot be overstated that how long it takes your child to master using the toilet has no bearing on his intelligence or success in any other area of his life. And it certainly doesn't reflect on your parenting abilities. Like all developmental milestones, your child will learn to use the toilet when he is ready, according to his own timetable. If you rush the process by starting him before he is emotionally or physically ready, you'll find yourself locked in a power struggle in which you're sure to lose one way or the other.

All through the teaching process, it's important that you monitor your own reactions to your child's progress. He may become resistant if you express either extreme pleasure when he does use the potty, or severe disappointment when he doesn't. Instead, use moderate praise and nonconfrontational reminders, such as "Next time, let's use the potty." If your child resists, back off for the time being, but stick to your routine. In time, your child will begin to see the benefits of using the potty.

You should also beware of putting subtle pressure on your child. Saying such things as "Don't you want to be a big boy [or girl]?" may backfire. Many two-year-olds are not so sure they're ready to grow up. And when your child has a lapse, he may feel as though he is a baby who failed an important test.

Be prepared for setbacks

Like most other developmental milestones, your child's toilet-learning does not progress in a straight line. Lapses are inevitable. When they occur, it's helpful to remember your child's early efforts at walking. Of course there were times when he fell, but you knew that eventually he would learn to be a confident walker, and you cheered him on. You would never have considered embarrassing him, scolding him, or punishing him for stumbling. So when your child does have a toileting lapse, keep in mind that he *wants* to be accomplished in toileting, but it just takes time for his skills to coordinate and become refined. Sometimes it's just that your child is so involved in an activity that he fails to notice his body's signals. It's not uncommon for children to have up to two incidents a day of wet pants.

No matter when, where, or how often your child has lapses, you should *never* punish him for his difficulties. It's hard not to feel angry or frustrated when your child doesn't seem to be getting the hang of it. You might even feel a mixture of anger and despair after he sits on the potty for five minutes, declares he doesn't have to go, then walks to the middle of your living room and urinates on the rug. But punishing your child will do more than make him feel bad about something over which he has little control; he may end up avoiding the potty altogether, and you'll be worse off than when you started teaching him.

Even if you suspect your child's accidents are deliberate, it's crucial that you not treat his lapses as a behavior problem. Instead, stay calm, and simply tell him that you and he need to clean up. Have him assist you in cleaning up urine from the floor. (But don't have him help you clean up any bowel movements; feces are laden with bacteria.) Ask him to help you gather some clean clothes and put the dirty ones in the hamper, and tell him in a matter-of-fact voice, "Next time, tell me when you have to use the potty so you can get there in time."

Did you know?

Summer weather is a great aid to toilet-teaching. You don't have the layers of clothes to deal with that you do in other seasons. Plus, you can put a potty outside where your two-year-old can easily get to it, and let him run around without a diaper. After a few times finding his feet and legs wet, he may make the connection between what his body produces and where it should be deposited.

When to ease up

Sometimes getting your child to give up diapers for good can take on an exaggerated importance, and you may find yourself acting in ways that are counterproductive to your child's learning process. Signs that you may be pushing too hard include getting angry at your child's toileting lapses, offering him big rewards for using the potty, forcing him to sit on the potty, and comparing his progress with that of other children.

Your child will also send you signals that it's time to ease up. If he withholds bowel movements, he may be reluctant to give up control. A normally outgoing child who suddenly becomes withdrawn may be feeling overly pressured to use the toilet. He may even hide from you to escape this pressure. Finally, if your child is having *no* success at using the potty, it's usually a sign that he's simply not ready. Discontinue toilet-teaching for a while, until he gives some indication that he's ready to learn.

Whatever your child's progress, your best approach is to remain patient, anticipate some ups and downs, and maintain your sense of humor. Whether it takes six weeks or six months, your child *will* eventually shed his diapers for good.

Learning to use the toilet is always a matter of taking two steps forward and one step back. Here are some common situations and the best way to handle them:

If your child...	Do say	Don't say
urinates in his pants while playing with a friend	"Next time, tell me when you have to use the potty so you can get there in time."	"What's the matter with you? You know better."
shows no interest in using the potty	Nothing. Your child may not be ready yet for toilet learning.	"Don't you want to be a big boy like Rob? He doesn't wear diapers anymore."
urinates on your living room rug after sitting on the potty for five minutes with no results	"Please take off your pants and put them in the hamper. Then I'm going to help you clean yourself and put on some fresh clothes."	"Look what you did! You're a bad boy!"
has been using the potty successfully for a while, but then has a series of lapses	"Oh, you didn't make it to the potty in time. I bet next time you will."	"You wet your pants—again? Do you want me to put you back in diapers?"

Toilet-teaching strategies

The keys to success in toilet-teaching are beginning slowly with no pressure, keeping your attitude low-key, and showing patience. While some children can learn to use the potty consistently in a matter of weeks, the process usually takes a few months.

Prepare your child before you start active teaching. Help your child become attuned to the feeling of the elimination process. You can do this by changing his diapers as soon as he wets or soils them so that he starts to develop a preference for clean, dry diapers. Teach him the concepts of "wet" and "dry" whenever the opportunity arises. For instance, if he spills juice, put his finger in the puddle and say "wet"; after you've wiped the surface, let him touch the same spot, and say "dry."

Help him become aware of the sensations of elimination. Be aware of when he's urinating or defecating by his body movements or facial expressions, such as suddenly stopping an activity, grimacing, or grunting. While this is happening say, "You're making a BM in your diaper," or, "Do you feel yourself getting wet and warm? That's because you're urinating."

Gradually introduce your child to using a potty chair. Because your child can sit in a potty chair with his feet firmly planted on the ground, he will most likely feel more secure than in using the toilet fitted with a child-sized lid. Some children are also frightened by the flushing of the toilet and may fear that they'll fall through.

Put the potty chair where it's easily accessible. Explain what it's used for, but don't make a big deal of it. Encourage your child to sit on it without undressing, so he can get used to it while still feeling the security of his diapers. If he happens to eliminate while sitting on the potty, don't try to get him out of the diaper. Simply point out to him what's happening so he can experience the sensation of urinating or having a bowel movement while sitting.

You might also encourage him to play a game with his dolls and stuffed animals in which he puts them on the potty. Dolls that wet are ideal for helping your child make the connection. It's also a good idea to let your child sit on the potty while you use the toilet. Or, while your child sits on the potty, read him a story about learning to use the toilet. Some recommendations:

♦ *I Have to Go* by Anna Ross (Random House, 1990)

♦ *No More Diapers* by J. G. Brooks, M.D. (Dell, 1989)

♦ *Once upon a Potty* by Alona Frankel (HarperCollins, 1999)

Finally, ask your child in a low-key way, "Would you like to try to use the potty, too?" This presents the idea as something new and exciting, as well as being something that your child *chooses* to do, not a task that's imposed on him.

Choose the time to start teaching wisely. You'll have greater success if you choose a quiet time in your child's life when he is not under stress. Such events as adjusting to a new sibling, a new home, a new sitter, a new school, or a change in schedule can all cause him to feel insecure and perhaps even regress. Plus, he simply won't have the emotional fortitude to learn. Wait until snowsuit season has passed, too.

Because you'll need to be most attentive to the learning process for the first week or two, you want to make sure that this is a convenient time for you, as well. It's a good idea to hold off teaching if you have any out-of-town trips or major events planned. Holidays are also not an ideal time to start because you'll probably feel too rushed or busy to give your child the attention and patience he needs. If you work outside the home, you might want to consider starting when you have a vacation.

Schedule regular potty times. By now you probably have a good idea of when your child tends to eliminate, usually after a nap or approximately 20 minutes after meals. Have your child sit on the potty during these times for a couple of minutes. Again, let him sit with his diaper on. If he eliminates while sitting, point out what's happening and praise his efforts without being too effusive. Overpraising can make your child inhibited about trying again.

The next step is to ask your child if he would like to try putting his BM (or whatever term you choose) in the potty. Generally, experts agree that it's best to focus on daytime toilet-learning before nighttime, which takes much longer to accomplish. When he's willing to try using the potty, let him do it without making a big fuss over it.

It may take a number of tries to get the timing just right, but eventually your child will have a bowel movement in the potty. When he does so, gently praise his efforts. This will encourage him to try again the next day. But don't expect him to tell you just yet when he's about to have a bowel movement. That takes some time for him to develop the sensation and coordination. For now, simply stick to your scheduled potty-sitting routine.

Since your child has most likely urinated while having a bowel movement, bladder training tends to go a lot quicker. However, you'll need to step up your potty sittings to every two hours or so. If you have a boy, it's best to start him off sitting. Make sure to remove the cuplike urine guard on your son's potty seat, as it can injure his penis. Teach him to aim his urine into the potty. As he gets older, he can begin to practice standing up while urinating. He'll learn best if he can watch his father, or other males, do it.

Make it easy for your child to get undressed. Because using the potty successfully can require split-second timing, give your child every opportunity for success. When you can, allow him to run around with a bare bottom. Training pants or pull-up diapers are usually easier to remove than regular diapers. And look for overpants with elasticized waists that can easily be pulled down. Girls can be helped through the process by wearing skirts or dresses.

If your child resists, back off. Avoid the temptation to offer your child rewards. Enjoying staying clean and dry should be its own reward. Besides, material rewards rarely work in the long run. Instead, let your child know that you're proud of him for his accomplishments and tell him you'll try again another day.

Teach your child good hygiene habits. It's important to teach your child to wipe himself on his own, though he probably won't get the hang of it until he reaches age three. Teach your child—especially girls—to wipe from the front to the back to help prevent urinary tract infections. Encourage your child to wipe gently to avoid irritating the skin and exposing it to infection. Uncircumcised boys should be taught to gently retract the foreskin before wiping after urinating. Make sure that your child knows that he must always wash his hands after using the toilet.

If your older two-year-old is resistant

Sometimes a child over the age of two-and-a-half shows all the signs of toilet readiness, but after several months of patient efforts by you, simply refuses to cooperate. Contrary to what you may think, this is not the time to get tough. Instead, you've got to ease off the teaching and try a different strategy.

Give your child responsibility for his own toileting. Have one last talk with your child about the subject of toilet-teaching. Tell him you can't help him anymore and that it's up to him whether or not he chooses to put his BM or urine in the potty. Tell him you will not remind him anymore to use the potty and that you know he understands what it is for. Make it clear that he is now fully in charge. Also be sure to refrain from talking to others about your child's toilet-learning when he's in earshot. Once he realizes there is nothing left to resist, your child may well begin using the potty on his own.

Create positive associations with the potty. You don't want to make sitting on the potty a punishment or something your child dreads—especially by forcing him to sit on it. A better approach is to let your child decorate his potty with stickers, if he likes. You might even use them as an incentive, by letting him put a sticker on every time he uses the potty successfully.

Give your child choices. Let him decide whether he wants to use the potty seat or the toilet fitted with a child-sized seat. Let him choose whether to wear regular diapers or the pull-up style. Offer cotton underpants, which, because they are far less absorbent than diapers, will increase his discomfort when he wets or has a BM. Be aware, of course, that accidents will, quite literally, spill over into other areas.

Enlist the help of others. Make sure your child's preschool or child-care provider follows the same strategies and that your child has easy access to the bathroom at day care. You might also ask another neutral adult, such as your child's pediatrician, a nurse, or teacher to talk to him about using the toilet.

Be patient. Eventually, your two-year-old will realize that it's preferable to stay clean and dry. It may seem like an eternity to you, but eventually all children get the hang of it.

Respect your child's uniqueness

All children develop at their own unique pace. It's your job to support and encourage your child's own natural schedule—and enjoy the ride!